GREEK DRAMA

GREEK DRAMA
IN ITS THEATRICAL
AND SOCIAL CONTEXT

PETER WALCOT

UNIVERSITY OF WALES PRESS
CARDIFF
1976

© University of Wales Press, 1976
ISBN 0 7083 0602 0

Printed in Wales by
CSP PRINTING LTD., ST. FAGAN'S ROAD
FAIRWATER, CARDIFF

To Bryn
who taught me so much and not only about Classics

Surely it is not merely all right but positively admirable to chance one's arm now and again? Surely it is more important to be occasionally right than never wrong?

E. J. Kenney, *New Frameworks for Old*

Contents

	page
Preface	ix
Poetic Drama and the Popular Audience	1
Length of Performance	11
The Spoken Word	22
Actors and Acting I	44
Actors and Acting II	59
Drama and Social Values	76
Drama and the Athenian Background	94
General Index	104
Index of Passages	107

Preface

Iт is obvious, I suppose, that the type and size of theatre in vogue when a play was written for the stage must be a crucial factor in determining the form assumed by that play, and certainly there has been no little discussion of the physical setting of the ancient theatre. Equally crucial is the influence of contemporary theatrical production, although here our evidence for the period before the fourth century B.C. is thin and difficult to interpret, and so less often examined. At the same time style of theatre and conditions of performance are part only of the jig-saw which we need to complete, if we wish to understand and appreciate Greek drama; it is my belief that the dramatic tradition which inspired the plays of Aeschylus, Sophocles and Euripides cannot be divorced from the totality of the cultural milieu of the age when their plays were conceived and first presented on the stage. But if we are to place Greek drama firmly in its cultural context, it is not sufficient to attempt a vague reconstruction of the historical and intellectual background of the fifth century B.C., and then to present such material as an introduction to a discussion of the plays in detail. We ought rather to commence with the plays themselves, investigating their theatrical context in the expectation that this will lead to a further investigation into their social context; this is the reason why in what follows I consider the production of a play in the fifth century B.C. and raise what may well seem at first sight an unimportant issue, asking how long it took to perform a play at the City Dionysia. I next proceed to a study of the supremacy of the spoken word in Athenian life, the art of the fifth-century actor, and the social values reflected in the plays of the Greek dramatists. Yet every playwright has need of an audience, and his original audience will illustrate the ideas and sentiments, the assumptions and prejudices, the interests and enthusiasms that had to be met if there were to be any hope of a favourable reception in the theatre. Therefore, my investigations open with an explicit study of the character of the Athenian audience and conclude by considering the national pride, verging on jingoism, so typical of classical Greece.

I accept that I pose questions more than I supply answers; my readers must often be content with suggestions, however much they may prefer established facts. Consolation, however, is afforded by the presumptuous thought that I follow the method of Plato's teacher, and what better example could there be than that offered by Socrates? If questions are asked which have been too long ignored, these are questions put to me frequently by undergraduates attending lectures and seminars at University

College, Cardiff as part of our courses on Greek literature in translation. My debt to these students who know no Greek but do know the work of the Elizabethan dramatists is considerable, though my greatest debt is owed to the person responsible for the introduction of what we at Cardiff have chosen to call 'Classical Studies'. I am certain that Doctor B. R. Rees will not resent his name being coupled with the host of anonymous students who were always his primary concern. The opinions which I express are my own and I accept full responsibility for them, but many, some consciously, others without realizing it, have contributed to their formation, and to all these I am sincerely grateful. I wish also to record my gratitude to the University of Wales Press and it officers for undertaking to publish this book at a time fraught with difficulties.

University College, Cardiff   P.W.
April 1975

Author's Note:— I have not attempted to be consistent in rendering the titles of Greek plays, preferring that name in common use today, e.g. *Seven against Thebes, Prometheus Vinctus, Oedipus Tyrannus, Hercules Furens, Iphigenia in Aulis.*

Poetic Drama and the Popular Audience

THE tragedies of Aeschylus, Sophocles and Euripides were first produced in fifth-century Athens. Although very nearly two thousand five hundred years have now passed since their original production, these plays continue to influence the dramatic tradition of Western Europe, and they remain the subject of critical acclaim and the source of personal pleasure. Since the beginning of the present century it has been increasingly appreciated that Greek drama can be understood only if it is firmly placed in its true context: Aeschylus, Sophocles and Euripides wrote their plays not for the reader who might ponder over a text in isolation and at leisure but for live spectators, sitting in a theatre and responding spontaneously to the combination of words and action presented on the stage. It is highly salutary that we are reminded, and reminded constantly, that the demands made by the theatre are different from those of the study, but we are all the victims of our own experience, and the experience which we share is one restricted to the theatre and theatrical production and performance as they exist or are practised today. It is with this thought in mind that I wish to point out that a knowledge of the contemporary theatre can be as dangerous as it can be helpful to the student of Greek drama, for it is tempting to stress similarities while overlooking crucial differences. The differences between the two forms of theatre, Greek and modern, are many, and one of the most significant of these is the difference in the type of audience frequenting the theatre today and the audience which packed itself into the Theatre of Dionysus at Athens in order to enjoy the latest play composed by the fifth-century tragedian.

It was festivals held in honour of the god Dionysus which provided the occasion for the production of the plays of Aeschylus, Sophocles and Euripides. The festivals were sponsored by the state and formed part of the annual calendar of religious ceremonies at Athens. The very fact that it was the state which organized the festivals suggests that the audience first witnessing these plays performed on the stage was no small, exclusive group or an élite, belonging to a particular social class, but formed what we may call a 'popular' audience in the sense that it was a body fully representative of the great mass of the Athenian people. A democratic state such as Athens would hardly be meeting its obligations, if it promoted what was aimed at satisfying the needs of a minority and not a substantial majority. Part of the cost of production of the plays, moreover, was defrayed by wealthier citizens, who undertook such a 'liturgy' as an act of public service, stressing again that the festivals at which plays were staged were public occasions. The other types of liturgies, and most obviously the trierarchy or maintenance of a trireme in the Athenian navy, reveal to us how essential these festivals were in the estimate of the Athenians.

The outstanding festival each year when Athens made provisions for dramatic entertainment was the City Dionysia, and at this festival plays were staged in the Theatre of Dionysus. The immense size by modern standards of the Theatre of Dionysus, which accommodated 14,000 or more spectators, confirms the opinion that audiences at Athens were not restricted, as they inevitably are in any modern theatre, to just one section of the total population. Theatre attendance today is essentially a middle-class habit, a fact which an architect takes into account when recommending the size of a new theatre; we build theatres seating hundreds rather than thousands. But popular audiences may still be found today: the difference in character between an ancient Greek audience and a modern theatre audience is the kind of difference which we would identify if we were to separate individual members of an average audience watching a film and an average audience watching a play at the Edinburgh Festival, for it has been the cinema and, more recently and even more extensively, television which have presided over the virtual extinction of popular entertainment in an actual theatre. The theatre of today is a minority interest, and it has been decades since the music hall, the 'illegitimate' stage, offered regular entertainment to a large and socially mixed section of the community. A sharp distinction may be drawn between the audience present in a theatre and the audience accustomed to watching a film or television, and such a distinction will be related to social class as much as to sheer numbers. This twofold difference is expressed most conveniently if we adopt the terminology of students of Elizabethan drama and use the words 'élite' and 'popular' to describe the two categories of audiences.[1]

It is obvious that the material handled by the dramatist and the way in which he treats that material will be conditioned to lesser or greater degree, and it is likely to be to a great extent, by the attitudes displayed by his audience. Few dramatists, however avant-garde, can afford to ignore, let alone defy, the sentiments and prejudices apt to be shared by the audience. Shock-therapy has its place in the modern theatre, but commercial success is also relevant. The Greek dramatist had a special reason for paying a strict regard to the feelings of the spectators: at the City Dionysia the playwrights were engaged in a competition, a prize being awarded to the 'best' dramatist each year. It is true that judges were appointed to make the award and these judges swore an oath to carry out their duties honestly, but at the same time the judges were not likely to be indifferent to the reactions, favourable or unfavourable, of the audience, for judges, no less than playwrights, must have been conscious of the presence of an audience and its applause or failure to applaud. What is really self-evident receives confirmation from a passage in Plato's *Laws* in which the speaker, an Athenian stranger, argues that a judge needs not only wisdom but especially courage, for the true judge ought not to bow to the dictates of the many or his own lack of education, nor ought he to betray the oath he took on being appointed judge because of cowardice. The judge's role is that of the teacher rather than that of the pupil of the spectators. The stranger goes on to deplore the law in Sicily and Italy which placed the verdict at the disposal of the spectators, claiming that this had ruined poets and spectators alike.[2] Philosphers are concerned with ideal situations, but dramatists with the living world of the theatre, and a wide gulf separates theory and practice. Inasmuch as Aeschylus, Sophocles and Euripides were writing for a popular audience and were hoping to win the approval and applause of a popular audience, we must not expect of them anything beyond the understanding and appreciation of such an audience.

If a scholar reads the text of a play but does not see the play actually being performed in a theatre, he is liable to become preoccupied with what he imagines are the ideas being expressed by the dramatist, and this was the fate of many critics in the nineteenth century. Such a tendency led to much speculation about the 'philosophy' of Aeschylus and his fellow dramatists, and this interest in ideas was reinforced by the traditional claim of the Greek poet to be rated a teacher of men. Philosophy addressed to a popular audience seems to represent a contradiction, for philosophy is something cultivated by the few but scarcely by the many comprising a mass audience. But our contradiction is more apparent than real, for it is characteristic of a popular audience that it should be 'prepared to be instructed and edified'.[3] We are inclined, moreover, to exaggerate the profundity of thought expressed by the tragedian. An illustration will reveal that my last statement is more than simply an opinion. The most obvious vehicle by means of which the Greek dramatist might attempt to instruct his audience is the chorus; a tragedy ends with a short statement from the chorus, and it is here, at the conclusion of the play, that one would anticipate finding a message, a final comment enabling the dramatist to hammer home to the listener the lesson to be learned from the theme of the play. The very fact, however, that the chorus makes so short a statement is indicative of the simplicity of any message. It is remarkable, furthermore, that four of the nineteen plays ascribed to Euripides to have survived to us, the *Alcestis, Andromache, Helen* and *Bacchae*, share the same five concluding verses, while a fifth play, the *Medea*, reproduces the last four of the verses, and the message here is simple even to the point of being trite: 'Many are the shapes of the divine ones, and many things do the gods bring about contrary to expectation; what was expected did not happen, but god found a way to achieve what was not expected. So this event has transpired.' Certainly this is a sentiment which a spectator, having seen any of the five plays performed, might well echo, but it is also a thought which is neither devastatingly novel nor subtle. Euripides does not qualify as the angry young man of the Greek theatre on the basis of the evidence offered by these lines, and the claim of any of the three tragedians to be classed as a 'philosopher' is dubious.

If the Greeks spoke of their poets as teachers, as Aristophanes, for example, does in the *Frogs*, we must remember how the Greek boy studied Homer and studied this author not for aesthetic reasons: Achilles offered a pattern for life whose influence was not restricted to Alexander the Great. The poets expressed the traditional values of Greek society, and, to some extent at least, reinforced as much as they illustrated such values. We shall discuss later the 'oral' character of Greek society, arguing that it was the spoken and not the written word which was the dominant means of communication among the Greeks. And in an oral culture, it has been argued, the theatre has an 'immense but informal educative function . . . as an institution serving to *remind* its members of accepted common values, and to confront them with a dramatic affirmation and confirmation of these'.[4]

The close of the *Alcestis* and the other plays mentioned above may be trite, but this does not mean that it is also ineffective. The chorus offers an apposite comment on a situation where the *peripeteia* or reversal of fortune is marked. This point has already been made and a further argument advanced: the close of these plays has been said to act as a final piece of ritual might act, and an analogy has been identified in the way in which the withdrawal of choir and clergy at the end of an Anglican church service is masked by a recessional hymn or organ voluntary. Hymn and organ are not mere conveniences but related to the service and integrated with the liturgy, and so are far from being superfluous or devoid of significance.[5] This argument and comparison have the additional merit of reminding us that the Athenians who celebrated the City Dionysia were partaking in a religious ceremony. The theatre in which the plays were presented stood within the sacred precinct of Dionysus; the plays themselves were performed in the very presence of the god and his priest, the former, of course, being represented by a cult statue. The god in whose honour the play was being staged might even appear as a member of the cast. We know four of the titles of the plays reputed to have been written by Thespis, the first of the Greek dramatists, and one of these titles, *Pentheus*, suggests that Dionysus could put in an appearance on the stage throughout the history of Greek drama. The chorus in the orchestra shows that no physical barrier separated performer from audience; the presence among the spectators of the cult statue of a god who might also be active on the stage further reveals that the absence of a physical barrier was matched by the absence of any 'spiritual' barrier. Stage, orchestra and auditorium formed a single unit and so too did actors, chorus and spectators, all of whom were sharing in a common act of devotion. We are forcibly reminded of this religious background by the interest in the aetiology of particular cults manifest in Greek tragedy: thus Aeschylus' *Oresteia* trilogy ends with the Furies made benevolent powers, the Eumenides or kindly ones, and their cult set up at Athens; by the close of Sophocles' *Oedipus Coloneus* Oedipus has received his tomb and achieved the status of hero; in his *Iphigenia in Tauris* Euripides makes a passing reference to the supposed origin of the ceremonies held on the second day of the Anthesteria festival (verses 958–60), and later, and at greater length, offers an aetiology for the cult of Artemis at Halae and for a second cult at Brauron (verses 1446ff.).

But the Greek tragedians were poets as well as dramatists. Poetic drama is not entirely absent from our own stage today, but it is a type of production which will attract only a small proportion of the already very small proportion of the present population which regularly visits the theatre. Of modern plays the one which perhaps most closely resembles a Greek tragedy in its structure is T. S. Eliot's *Murder in the Cathedral*, consisting, as it does, of a series of episodes divided from one another by choral odes.[6] Its author has commented on the audience for which his play was originally written: it was, in Eliot's own words, 'a rather special kind of audience— an audience of those serious people who go to "festivals" and expect to have to put up with poetry . . . it (that is, the play) was a religious play, and people who go deliberately to a religious play at a religious festival expect to be patiently bored and to satisfy themselves with the feeling that they have done something meritorious.'[7] It is a fair guess that Eliot had his tongue held firmly in his cheek when he passed this comment, and it is true that *Murder in the Cathedral* established rather than followed a fashion. Yet it is equally true that Eliot abandoned the chorus in its basic form in his later plays and preferred a contemporary setting for his characters: *The Cocktail Party*, for instance, has been called a verse play which looks very much like a prose play, and at the time of its composition and production its title had a decidedly fashionable ring. Concessions had to be made when West End managers took over from festival organizers. Eliot proved a box-office success, and so also did Christopher Fry, who shares with the Greek tragedians a love for verbal pyrotechnics and luxuriant language on the stage, a vitality of dialogue which compensates for an apparent lack of action, a preference for traditional subject-matter yielding a simple plot, a tendency to let what does happen on the stage be unusual and startling, and a strong sense of religious conviction. But Eliot and Fry do not represent a dominant trend in the living theatre and their success in the forties and fifties still leaves us faced with a seeming paradox—in fifth-century Athens poetic drama could be enjoyed by a popular audience, whereas today it is merely an élite within an élite which is prepared to tolerate this type of production. Why should this be the situation? Can any explanation be suggested which avoids the absurdity of our crediting the Athenians with what some appear to regard as an almost divinely inspired intellectual superiority? The fact that poetic drama was welcomed enthusiastically by the popular audiences which attended the public theatres of Elizabethan England implies that a more convincing answer ought to be forthcoming.

The success of Fry was greeted warmly by Rudolf Stamm, who saw in it encouraging evidence of a revolt against realism in modern English drama.[8] For this critic realistic drama was one species of play and poetic drama another, quite distinct species, and it had been the former type of play which had dominated the theatre for decades. It is difficult but challenging to attempt a definition of the essential character of Greek tragedy, but the negative definition 'non-realistic' has its adherents. Others will rightly prefer a positive statement of what Greek drama is rather than what it is not, and it is the various conventions present in a Greek play— the chorus, use of verse, messenger speech, and here I list only the most obvious with no effort to be comprehensive—which will suggest an alternative definition, and so we soon find ourselves ranging on the one side the realism of the modern theatre and on the other the conventions typifying Greek drama. But in doing this have we in fact escaped the dangers of a negative definition? Surely we tend to think of a convention not as a standard way in which something is done but as a non-realistic way in which something is done. We forget that a convention may be the result of tradition, although this is blatantly obvious in the case, for example, of the Greek chorus, and rather ascribe conventions indiscriminately to convenience, arguing, and again I choose an obvious example, that the Greeks were incapable of depicting violent action convincingly on the stage, and that, therefore, a convention developed whereby action was thought to take place off-stage and then reported on stage by a messenger-type character. We impose, in other words, an arbitrary standard derived from the realistic tradition of our own theatre on the Greeks and assume that inability rather than calculated choice shaped the conventions characterizing Greek drama. Convention then becomes a limitation and even an embarrassment and the theatrical tradition which features conventions an inferior kind of drama. Yet the lavish praise we shower on the Greek theatre and on the Elizabethan theatre, which was similarly characterized by a set of conventions, contradicts this consequence of the attitude which we so often adopt towards conventions. Experience of the contemporary cinema will suggest that it is realism which commands the interests of a popular audience today, and keeping this in mind we may rephrase the question put in our preceding paragraph: Why should so few today but so many in fifth-century Athens accept and apparently enjoy non-realistic drama? The easy and, I think, the correct answer is a reply that the Greeks were not conscious that their dramas were 'non-realistic' or in any way not true to life. Having no knowledge of the theatre of Ibsen and Chekhov, they were prepared to accept where we are only too willing to question. Our question is not a valid one, for it requires us to speak of absolutes when we refer to realistic and non-realistic drama, but such absolutes do not exist. Real life cannot be reproduced in the theatre with absolute fidelity, whatever technical resources we may have at our disposal. Or, if we wish to be more subtle, we may say with Raymond Williams that 'what is called conventional, in the sense of an old routine, is a method or set of methods which present a different kind of action, and through it a different kind of reality'.[9] And the philosophers of the Greeks themselves have taught us that anything which is seen or heard is in one sense real; on the other hand, all drama is an imitation, and an imitation must represent a lower level of reality than that which it imitates.

The technical resources of the cinema should enable a film, something recorded and subsequently edited before it is shown to an audience, to be realistic to an extent denied the producer within a theatre, whose ambitions must necessarily be curtailed by the physical limitations of the theatre. In a theatre we are encapsulated within a closed environment, whereas the camera may exploit an out-of-door setting. A film may be consistently 'real', or so we think. But consider one of the standard genres in the cinema, the Musical. In the thirties and to a lesser extent in the forties, Musicals tended to be centred about the young and aspiring cast of a play or show written by a brilliant but unknown author; recently the plot of the Musical has been much more grim, and grimness suggests the real world. A Pacific island threatened by Japanese invasion or a Nazi-dominated Europe is a setting not unrelated to contemporary world events. It has remained a convention of such productions, however, that, at the slightest excuse, characters may burst into song without apparently breaking the illusion of reality or in any way unsettling the audience. Even the Western, a type of film heavily dependent on an out-of-door setting, creates an impression of reality which any serious scrutiny could easily shatter. A film must not run for more than ninety minutes or two hours, and within this brief span of time it must compress what in real life may

drag on over the course of several years. What is exciting, what is dramatically effective is extrapolated, for real life is too slow, too ordinary, too
tedious to offer consistent entertainment. If one were invited to list all the
conventions of Greek drama, that list, I suspect, would be incomplete,
because certain conventions are conventions which are also accepted in
our own theatres and cinemas and are, therefore, not recognized for what
they always have been and still are—Persians speak Greek in Aeschylus
and Red Indians speak English in a Western film, the language which is
intelligible to the audience always having been decisive in creating this
convention. Today we realize that Greek drama was written to be performed on a stage and not to be read by an individual; to draw upon our
own experience in the theatre, whether as producer or as member of the
audience, as was said before, is most helpful if too academic an approach
is to be avoided. But at the same time we must remember that we are
living in the twentieth century A.D. Just as a modern producer is inclined
to introduce a modern 'message', something of immediate relevance, into
a Greek play, seeing the *Trojan Women* as a commentary on the Vietnam
conflict or the *Bacchae* as propaganda for Women's Liberation, so also
this producer uses, and what is more, is entitled to use, the resources now
available in a theatre. The contemporary actor has been trained in a certain
tradition and cannot be expected to unlearn what it has probably taken
him years of patient effort to master. Finally, the spectator has been conditioned by a type of drama which he has seen much more often than he
has seen a modern production of a Greek play; he will expect an approxi-
mation to reality as the usual style in which a play is presented on the stage.

It can, moreover, be shown to be very likely that Greek drama, in spite
of its being poetic drama, did reproduce real life in the eyes of those who
first saw these plays. In Aristophanes' comedy the *Acharnians* the hero of
the play, Dicaeopolis, visits the house of Euripides to borrow some items
from the poet's wardrobe of beggar's rags in order to plead the cause of
peace more effectively (verses 393ff.). The scene yields a golden opportunity for Aristophanes to pour ridicule on the head of Euripides because
of his fondness for dressing his beggar-heroes in tatters. This form of prop,
of course, in itself reveals some feeling for the realistic presentation of
character on the Greek stage. But the passage has more evidence to offer us.
The door of the house is opened by an underling who proceeds to indulge
in the type of verbal quibble associated with his master: Euripides, it
seems, is both in and not in—in other words, he is at home but his mind
is abroad culling snippets of poetry. Euripides is at home writing a tragedy
anabaden (verses 399), an adverb whose basic meaning is 'with his feet up'.
Is this detail significant? I think it is, for Euripides specialized in beggar-
heroes who were not only dressed in rags but were also lame. When the

poet is trundled on the stage on the *eccyclema*, some kind of wheeled platform,[10] Dicaeopolis passes the following remark: 'Are you composing with your feet up when you could do it with your feet down? No wonder your characters are lame. Why are you wearing tragic rags, clothes so wretched? No wonder your characters are beggars' (verses 410–13). The implication of these verses, however good a joke they also are, is that the poet Euripides, when writing a part for one of his lame beggars, 'thought' himself into the role as much as he possibly could by assuming the appropriate dress and manner. The character was 'real' to the dramatist and this is a good guarantee that it was no less real to the audience. Aristophanes is cracking a joke and it is a good joke which bears repetition, and it is repeated in a later comedy, the *Thesmophoriazusae*, when another dramatist, Agathon, is depicted dressed up in woman's clothes when writing the part of a woman. The joke here, furthermore, has a second dimension in view of Agathon's sexual proclivities, but, while jokes are jokes, they cease to be funny if they are too far divorced from the truth. In this second comedy Mnesilochus tries to help his relative Euripides by insinuating himself among the women celebrating the Thesmophoria festival, who are plotting to destroy the poet. A disguise is needed as women alone were admitted to these rites, and Euripides would have Mnesilochus borrow female attire from Agathon. The incident which interests us follows the same pattern as the corresponding event in the *Acharnians*. The door of Agathon's house is opened by a servant whose language betrays the influence of his master (verses 39ff.). When Agathon comes onto the stage it is on the *eccyclema* (see verses 96 and 265), but he is not recognized at first by Mnesilochus who thinks he is looking at a woman (verse 98). Why, Mnesilochus asks, is Agathon dressed like a woman to the extent of wearing the full range of feminine clothes (verses 136ff.): all he appears to lack is a physical attribute, breasts. Agathon's reply is succinct and to the point (verses 148–52):

> I dress by the drift of my thoughts. You see,
> a dramatic poet must submit
> to *all* the demands of his characters—
> so, if he writes about women he must
> dress like a woman, and *be* a woman.[11]

If Agathon's personal wishes happen to coincide with his needs as a poet, a special quality is added to the joke. But what is of immediate concern to us is the fact that it appears that Euripides and Agathon, according to Aristophanes, lived the roles they created, and so were fulfilling the advice offered the dramatist later by Aristotle in the *Poetics*: 'In composing plots and working them out so far as verbal expression goes, the poet should, more than anything else, put things before his eyes, as he then sees the events most vividly as if he were actually present, and can therefore find what is appropriate and be aware of the opposite . . . So far as possible one should also work it out with the appropriate figures. For given the same natural endowment, people who actually feel passion are the most convincing; that is, the person who most realistically expresses distress is the person in distress and the same is true of a person in a temper' (1455a 22–32).[12]

On the basis of the evidence available in Aristophanes and of the advice contributed by Aristotle, I would argue that Greek plays reproduced real life in the assessment of the Greeks. They may not be realistic by our standards, but then our standards are meaningless if applied rigorously to drama which was first produced nearly two and a half millennia ago. They were real enough, I would repeat, real enough to those who saw the original performance, and these spectators are what is actually important to a playwright taking part in a competition with the hope of carrying off the first prize. Much of what follows in the subsequent chapters will be concerned with the nature of reality in the theatre and the effectiveness of conventions. If the first question posed and discussed in detail—How long did it take to perform a play in antiquity?—appears to be far removed from the subject of reality as it was recognized by the Greek playgoer, it will eventually be seen to have a bearing on our major interest and, from the very beginning, will stress the folly of any assumption based on a belief that the production and performance of plays in antiquity was closely related to what happens in the theatre today. There are, of course, similarities but these have been too frequently emphasized at the expense of differences which are not less worthy of a critic's attention.

NOTES
1 The two types of audience are admirably described and considered by Alfred Harbage, *Shakespeare and the Rival Traditions* (New York, 1952). The popular audience and television drama have recently been studied by J. S. R. Goodlad, *A Sociology of Popular Drama* (London, 1971). That the common man is uncommon in theatre audiences is revealed by the surveys conducted by William J. Baumol and William G. Bowen as reported in Elizabeth and Tom Burns (edd.), *Sociology of Literature and Drama* (Penguin Modern Sociology Readings, 1973), pp. 445–70.
2 Plato, *Laws* 659a–c. That the aim of tragedy was to please the audience above all else is made clear by the *Gorgias* 502b.
3 I quote from the description of the Elizabethan popular audience offered by M. C. Bradbrook, *The Growth and Structure of Elizabethan Comedy* (London, 1955), pp. 7–8: 'The Elizabethan audience, rowdy, vocal, sometimes dangerous, far more conscious of its unity, far better acquainted and more unified than the modern audience, was also prepared to be instructed and edified. It came with a very definite set of moral expectations, with which both players and playwrights were familiar.' That the chorus is not to be considered a vehicle for philosophy nor the poets philosophers is argued by Brian Vickers, *Towards Greek Tragedy: Drama, Myth, Society* (London, 1973), pp. 12ff. and 64ff.
4 Terence Hawkes, *Shakespeare's Talking Animals, Language and Drama in Society* (London, 1973), p. 125.
5 See B. R. Rees, *American Journal of Philology* 82 (1961), pp. 176–81.
6 See David E. Jones, *The Plays of T. S. Eliot* (London, 1960), pp. 51ff.
7 The comment was passed in a lecture 'Poetry and Drama' originally published separately in 1951 and reprinted in *On Poetry and Poets* (London, 1957), p. 79.
8 *Anglia* 72 (1954), pp. 78–109.
9 *Drama in Performance* (London, 1968), p. 178.
10 The use of *eccyclema* is implied by the occurrence in verse 408 and verse 409 of the corresponding verb *eccyclein*.
11 I quote the translation by Patric Dickinson, *Aristophanes Plays 2* (Oxford, 1970).
12 The translation of the *Poetics* quoted throughout is that by M. E. Hubbard, published in D. A. Russell and M. Winterbottom (edd.), *Ancient Literary Criticism, the Principal Texts in New Translations* (Oxford, 1972).

Length of Performance

If a production of a Greek play is contemplated today, one is faced with innumerable problems. Many of these problems will be peculiar to the individual producer and his own production, but there is, in addition, no lack of difficulties with which any impresario will have to grapple, irrespective of the competence of his cast, the facilities offered by his theatre, or the lavishness of funds to be disposed. Although seldom mentioned, much less stressed, one of the most intractable of problems is set by the length of an ancient drama: the Greek play, whether it be tragedy or comedy, is simply not long enough to meet the expectations of a modern audience, that is, its expectations in terms of duration of performance. We expect to be entertained in the theatre for something like two and a half hours or more; even when allowance is made for one or possibly two intervals, at least two hours of action on the stage is for us the norm. Professional actors are equipped by training and by experience to control the pace of performance; they, however, are hard pressed to present a version of a Greek play which will conform to anything like such a norm. The choral odes offer the greatest scope for extended treatment, but here also what may be done is restricted by the need to safeguard the balance of the play. It is possible that audiences are more sympathetic when watching an amateur production, but I do not believe that it is merely an occasional member of the audience who, having seen the curtain rise on a production of Greek tragedy at 7.30 p.m. and fall very shortly after 9.00 p.m., has suffered a sense of frustration. To turn to an actual case, was Victor Martin, the first modern editor of Menander's *Dyskolos*, the only member of the audience to be struck by the short duration of time required for the play's performance, particularly when this comedy was presented at Epidaurus, in Greece itself, in 1960—'one thing had struck him: some of these productions, particularly that at Epidaurus in 1960, had only lasted with difficulty for more than a half-hour.'[1] Admittedly, the *Dyskolos* is a brief play, being less than a thousand lines long and it includes no words specially written for a chorus, but in several ways its performance at Epidaurus provides an excellent test: the play was staged by Greeks, that is, those whose native tongue is Greek, in a restored Greek theatre; inasmuch as Menander did not compose special songs for the chorus, imponderable factors, such as the music and dance which accompanied the words of the chorus, do not complicate the issue. And what was the reaction of the spectator to seemingly so abrupt a production? The play, it is claimed, turned out to be mutilated; reduced to the dimensions of a

'lever de rideau', it made little impact on its audience. Yet, in spite of
Victor Martin's misgivings, there is nothing intrinsically wrong with a
play which lasts for only about thirty minutes; indeed such productions
are standard fare for the television viewer. The production of the *Dyskolos*
at Epidaurus represents one extreme; the other extreme, a performance
lasting nearly two hours, staged to celebrate the fifth centenary of the
University of Bâle, also had its limitations, the rhythm of the action
clearly being too slow.

A filmed version of a Greek play may be surprisingly effective, for we
do not feel ourselves to be deceived if the film runs for just ninety minutes,
and the director of a film, moreover, can legitimately exploit the great
asset of his medium: the camera may feature the desolate, bleak hills of
Greece, presenting a series of visual images which, however much time
they consume, seem to supplement rather than to impede the action. What
was achieved by verbal description in the original production the film
achieves visually. Thus in the opening speech of the *Electra* Sophocles'
paidagogos refers to the 'sights' of Argos (verses 4ff.). The reference is
brief, as such references are in Greek tragedy, but, since this type of
comment, slight though it may be, would have been reinforced in antiquity
by a knowledge, both personal and traditional, which served to stimulate
the imagination of the Greek audience, the film director may claim some
justification here for the supplement provided by his camera. Furthermore,
the setting of the open-air Greek theatre is more evocatively suggested
by a filmed version than by a production confined within the proscenium-
arch type theatre still normal today. Running on the average for only
ninety minutes, the film dispenses with any interval and in this way avoids
the dangerous consequences of splitting a Greek drama into segments.
Above all else, we recognize that the cinema is a different medium and are,
therefore, not seduced into believing, as we inevitably are in the theatre,
that we are witnessing a performance approximating to that of the play's
first production.

It must not be assumed that it took as long to perform a play in antiquity as it takes to stage the same play today, and even less must we
assume that a play performed in an ancient theatre ran for as long as an
average play in its modern counterpart. Yet the second assumption,
although its absurdity appears to be blatant, is made: thus one scholar,
speaking of the actors at the City Dionysia, remarks, 'With short intervals
only, they had therefore to perform in one day three tragedies and one
satyr play, which meant that they had to be in harness for at least ten
hours'.[2] This opinion presumably allows not far short of, if not more than,
three hours for the performance of each tragedy. In the fifth century B.C.
during the period of the Peloponnesian War, on each of three successive

days at the City Dionysia, three tragedies, a satyr play and a comedy
were performed. If a contemporary producer were to stage on the same
day five contemporary plays, he would require his audience to be present
in the theatre for considerably more than ten hours; perhaps he might be
able to squeeze everything, the plays themselves and an occasional break,
into a period of twelve hours. But how long is it likely to have taken to
stage the three tragedies, one satyr play and one comedy at the City
Dionysia?

Firm evidence enabling us to answer the question posed above once and
for all would be offered only a definite statement by a reliable ancient
authority, and such evidence we do not possess and cannot expect to
recover. Obsession with time, the need to distinguish between one minute
before the hour and one minute after the hour, is a modern preoccupation
which the Greeks were fortunate not to share. Their devices for measuring
time, the *gnomon, heliotropion, clepsydra*, were unsophisticated and the
terms used to denote a particular hour notoriously vague—'the time when
the market is full', 'the hour when oxen are released', 'the hour of lighting
the lamps'; a word like *deile* can mean the beginning as well as the end of
the afternoon.[3] Modern critics who discuss the programme of events at
the City Dionysia do not quote precise figures in terms of hours, but the
opinion of the standard authorities, in spite of that omission, is perfectly
clear. Early in this century Haigh stated that 'the performance of plays
began soon after sunrise, and continued all day long without inter-
mission . . . It is manifest that, considering the large number of plays which
had to be gone through in the time, any delay would have been out of the
question.'[4] Gould and Lewis refer to 'performances going on continuously
from dawn to evening'.[5] No evidence is cited to confirm the belief that
performances continued very late in the day. As Gould and Lewis themselves note elsewhere, that the ceremonies of the day, but not the plays,
began at dawn is suggested by Aeschines and Demosthenes,[6] though one
is entitled to wonder, when Dicaeopolis' complaint in the *Acharnians* of
Aristophanes is remembered (verses 19ff.), how prompt a start was regularly the rule. The early start at the City Dionysia (or possibly the reference
is one to the Rural Dionysia), Gould and Lewis add, is referred to by
Xenophon,[7] but the passage—'I know', says Socrates, 'that to see comedies
you get up very early and go very long distances'—suggests that some
account ought to be taken of the time spent by what was an immensely
large audience in travelling from home to the theatre (and also in returning
home from the theatre later in the day).

But now we are beginning to speculate, when there are facts which
remain available to us. It was the ceremonies of the day and not the actual
plays which seem to have commenced at dawn. How these ceremonies

were arranged—Were they spread over the three days of dramatic entertainment or concentrated on one or, in some cases, repeated?—we do not
know, but we do know that these ceremonies in the fifth century were no
trifling procedures of a kind to be rushed. This is how Haigh describes
them:

> During the period of the actual contests the audience met in the theatre every
> morning soon after daybreak. Considering the number of plays which had to be
> produced, it was necessary that the proceedings should begin at an early hour. The
> vast gathering of spectators, like all public meetings at Athens, was first of all
> purified by the offer of a small sacrifice. Then libations were poured in front of the
> statue of the god Dionysus. If the festival were the City Dionysia, *before the tragedies
> began* (my own italics) the opportunity was taken to proclaim the names of citizens
> upon whom crowns had been bestowed, together with the services for which they
> had been granted. The proclamation before such a vast multitude of citizens was
> naturally considered a very great honour. During the period of Athenian supremacy
> another striking ceremony preceeded the tragedies at the City Dionysia. The tribute
> collected from the dependent states was divided into talents, and solemnly deposited
> in the orchestra. Then the orphans whose fathers had been killed in battle, and who
> had been educated by the state, and had now reached the age of manhood, were
> brought forward upon the stage equipped in complete armour. The herald made a
> proclamation, recounting what the state had done for them and they were then
> publicly discharged from state control to take their place as ordinary citizens. *After
> these preliminaries had been gone through the dramatic performances commenced.*[8]

Striking ceremonies, and this is how Haigh describes them, constitute
more than mere 'preliminaries', and one is left to deduce that Haigh,
mistakenly obsessed by what he thought to be pressure of time, chose the
word preliminaries so as to avoid too glaring an inconsistency with his
belief that 'the performance of plays began soon after sunrise'. Notice
how he begs the question when he remarks 'considering the number of
plays which had to be produced'. But the size of the separate units con-
tributes as much to the total as the number of these units and, as we shall
see, Greek plays are short. The display of tribute when at least five hundred
men paraded through the orchestra, each carrying one talent of money,
must have been a spectacular sight, but the other ceremonies were not
devoid of splendour, and surely we should allow a generous allocation of
time for every one of them. In addition, it has been argued that the parade
of tribute was introduced between the death of Pericles and the performance of Aristophanes' comedy the *Babylonians*, that is, between 428 and
426 B.C. or early in the Peloponnesian War when dramatic performance
at the City Dionysia was restricted to three days.[9] Even, it seems, a
restricted programme was not so tight as to prevent a considerable addition
to the accompanying procedures.

The time consumed in the performance of a play is obviously related to
the length of the play. Where our evidence, factual though it may be, is

limited by the accident of survival, caution is to be exercised and unknown factors borne in mind constantly. Do our surviving texts, for example, accurately reproduce what was acted on the stage at the original performance or even a standard performance later? One's confidence is shaken when it is found that in the *Frogs* Aristophanes quotes the opening verses of Aeschylus' *Choephori* (verses 1126–28 and 1172–73), lines which are preserved by none of our manuscripts of the tragedian. Another problem is illustrated by the various revisions thought to be embodied in our present text of the *Clouds*—Was this comedy, as we possess it, ever intended for the stage? Again, there is the more general question of actors' interpolations —Is the end of the *Seven against Thebes* actually by Aeschylus? It so happens that we have in our possession today texts of over forty plays written by Aeschylus, Sophocles, Euripides and Aristophanes. If a member of the general public were to be asked how texts of these Greek plays have survived the passage of some two thousand five hundred years, our average man or woman would probably profess a pardonable ignorance. A person who had received a classical education is likely to say something or other about manuscripts, adding that these ultimately go back to editions compiled by scholars working in Hellenistic Alexandria. Yet this period of literary scholarship was removed by more than a century from the period of time when the Athenian dramatists flourished and much could, and apparently did, happen during such a stretch of time, for in 330 B.C. it was ordered that a public copy of the text of the three great tragedians be placed in the state archives in order to provide an authorized text for actors to use (Plutarch, *Vit. X orat.* 841 F). The evidence of the *Frogs*, a comedy in which the god Dionysus, posing as an intellectual, claims to have been reading the *Andromeda* of Euripides while on active service with the fleet (verses 52–53), reveals that texts of tragedies circulated in the fifth century B.C., but we know nothing of the process by which a dramatist produced a script for use in the theatre when the first performance of a particular play was in preparation, nor anything of the process by which a document like a script made its way into the hands of a 'publisher'.

But leaving problems such as those mentioned above on one side, I wish to ask whether the length of the individual tragedies and the satyr play produced on the same day varied, but added up to roughly the same total every day. Our solitary example of an extant trilogy, the *Oresteia*, amounts to 3796 verses (Shakespeare's *Hamlet* is of an almost identical length, but is an exceptionally long play by Shakespearean standards), but its first element, the *Agamemnon*, makes up 1673 of these. If we exclude the *Agamemnon*, the tragedies of Aeschylus are as remarkably uniform as they are remarkably short in length, varying from the 1047 verses of the

Eumenides to the 1093 verses of the *Prometheus Vinctus* or the 1078 verses of the *Seven against Thebes* if the *Prometheus Vinctus* is to be excluded on the grounds that its first performance took place outside Athens. The variation, therefore, is slight, being less than fifty lines. At the same time Aeschylus' satyr drama the *Dictyulci* seems to have been considerably longer than our only completely extant play of this type, the *Cyclops* of Euripides (709 verses).[10] The *Alcestis*, the fourth play of a tetralogy, conforms more to the standard length of a tragedy, consisting of 1163 verses. If we ignore the posthumously produced *Oedipus Coloneus*, which totals 1779 verses, the tragedies of Sophocles range from the 1278 verses of the *Trachiniae* to the 1530 verses of the *Oedipus Tyrannus*, the average length of the six plays being 1427 lines. If we extract the *Cyclops* and the *Alcestis* and ignore the probably mutilated *Heraclidae* and the probably spurious *Rhesus*, the remaining fifteen plays ascribed to Euripides average out at approximately 1474 verses or 1469 verses if we also delete the posthumously produced *Bacchae* and *Iphigenia in Aulis*, the two extremes being provided by the *Phoenissae* of 1766 and the *Supplices* of 1234 verses. The average for both Sophocles and Euripides, then, is greater than for Aeschylus. Although eleven comedies by Aristophanes survive, our evidence here is thinner than one suspects. There is a pronounced divergence in length between the longest, the *Birds* at 1765 verses, and the shortest, the *Ecclesiazusae* at 1183 verses, of the comedies of Aristophanes; their average length of 1390 verses is increased by some forty lines if we ignore the two comedies dating from the fourth century B.C., as presumably we ought in view of the gradual displacement of songs specially written for the chorus by the playwright. There is a further complication: only the *Clouds* (1511 verses), *Peace* (1357 verses) and the *Birds* are known to have been produced for the City Dionysia, whereas the *Acharnians*, *Knights*, *Wasps* and *Frogs* were staged at another festival, the Lenaea.

At first glance there appears to be meagre consistency in the figures I have quoted, a fact in itself, it might be argued, which suggests that the time-table of performances at the City Dionysia was not as hectic as is frequently assumed. The solid piece of information is offered by the *Oresteia* trilogy, since in this case we know that the three tragedies presented on one and the same day amounted to a total of some 3800 lines of verse. If such a total can be accepted as a regular figure *circa* 460 B.C., some sense may be made of the apparent confusion, or some sense at least relating to the three tragedies produced on the same day. If it were not a trilogy but three tragedies, each an independent work not linked in theme, which formed the major element of a day's entertainment in the Theatre of Dionysus, it may be conjectured that the three plays taken together would equal the total length of the *Oresteia* and probably go somewhat beyond that total as the fifth century progressed. If each of the three tragedies produced on the same day was a self-contained unit and unable to draw upon and to exploit a knowledge derived from the proceeding drama or dramas, we would expect the plays to be of an uniform length unlike the plays of the *Oresteia* trilogy where the *Agamemnon* is so much longer than the two plays which follow it. But at this point the almost inevitable caveat must be entered; the only surviving play by Aeschylus which we know not to have been part of a trilogy is the *Persae*, and the *Persae* totals only 1077 verses and is, therefore, of approximately the same length as this playwright's other extant dramas with the exception, of course, of the *Agamemnon*. At the same time the *Persae* is our earliest tragedy, being the second play in the sequence of three tragedies presented by Aeschylus in 472 B.C.

The evidence offered by the *Oresteia* and the average figures quoted above, 1427 for a drama by Sophocles and 1474 for a drama by Euripides, suggest that each tragedy, as the fifth century went on, was at least 1250 lines in length and even considerably, say 250 lines plus, longer. When the trilogy became fashionable once again in the last quarter of the fifth century, the practice of presenting plays of a similar length would have been firmly established, and so the *Trojan Women* of Euripides, which was the third member of a trilogy comprising the *Alexander, Palamedes* and the *Trojan Women*, totals 1332 lines and suggests a length for the complete trilogy of about 4000 or more verses. We know that the three tragedies produced on one day of the City Dionysia of 458 added up to a total of 3796 verses; our, admittedly uncertain, evidence implies that this total of verses grew with the continuation of the fifth century, but it is unlikely to have grown to much in excess of 4500 verses. If we now add to our possible maximum of 4500 verses the equivalent of a satyr play and a comedy—erring on the side of generosity, we may allow some 2500 verses —we have a grand total for a day of 7000 verses, although a figure some 500 verses lower is perhaps a more convincing estimate. Thus, if we take the average for a Euripidean tragedy and multiply this calculation by three, then attach the 709 verses of the *Cyclops*, and finally allow 1430, our Aristophanic fifth-century average, the resultant formula is $(1474 \times 3) + 709 + 1430$ or a total of 6561 verses for each day of dramatic entertainment at the time of the Peloponnesian War.

The three plays making up the *Oresteia* are not unlike the three acts of a single production; they can be, and indeed benefit from being, performed continuously with merely a short break between each play interrupting the action on the stage. A short break would seem to be required, for example, to permit the chorus to change costume: it is elders of Argos who comprise the chorus of the *Agamemnon*, women in mourning the chorus of the *Choephori*, and the Furies the chorus of the *Eumenides*. There is no reason, however, why we ought to assume that this break was anything other than the shortest of intervals, whether the tragedies being performed formed a trilogy or were three plays distinct in contents. The assumption that there was more than a brief respite between the individual tragedies really depends for its acceptance upon a second assumption and an assumption, moreover, which I am attempting to challenge, namely that each particular play took a considerable time to perform and the audience, therefore, needed more of a break. The capacity of the audience in a modern theatre is no guide to the tolerance of its fifth-century equivalent, for, as we saw in the preceding chapter, the modern audience is an élite, far removed in character from the popular audience jammed into the theatre at Athens on a series of days given over to celebrating the glory of a god. Our experience of the cinema, with its 'double-feature' programme and a break only in the sense that the main films give way to advertisement and 'shorts', reveals that a popular audience is quite capable of sitting through a programme of virtually continuous entertainment.

According to a passage in Aristophanes' *Birds* one advantage of possessing wings is said to be an ability to fly off home and to take the mid-day meal when hungry and bored with the tragedies and then to return with full stomach to watch the comic performance (verses 786–89). On the basis of this passage and its reference to the mid-day meal (*eristesen* in verse 788), Gould and Lewis state 'that in 414 B.C. comedies were acted in the afternoons of the same days as were devoted to tragedies'.[11] As they also subscribe to the view that the dramatic entertainment went on until evening, are we to credit them with a belief that the tragedies still carried on after mid-day, lasting so long in fact that the following satyr play and comedy were not completed until evening? Yet if it was just the combination of satyr play and comedy which remained to be performed after mid-day, how can entertainment on the stage have carried on as late as the arrival of evening? Another scholar considers the passage from the *Birds* as evidence for the presentation of tragedies and 'afterpiece', that is, satyr play in the morning and a single comedy in the afternoon, an even thinner programme for the period after mid-day and one which could certainly not last until evening, however much time is allowed for the greater element of stage-business demanded by comedy.[12] And a second reference in the *Birds* may serve to confirm the theory that the tragedies and satyr play were completed by mid-day and it was just the comedy which occupied what must have been only part of the afternoon, thus leaving the spectators with sufficient time at their disposal to return safely to what in some cases surely were quite scattered homes. Late in the comedy when the city of Cloudcuckooland has been founded and the gods subjected to blockade, Prometheus comes on stage to urge that the birds continue with their siege of the gods. The Titan cowers under a 'parasol' to prevent his being spotted by Zeus from above and shows signs of great agitation. Anxious to escape detection, he asks the time of day and receives a clear and direct enough answer—'it's a little after mid-day' (verses 1498–99). A joke is a joke, and the reply given Prometheus may be nothing more than part of a comic situation, but this joke gains an added element of humour if in this instance we are able to argue for a coincidence of actual time and dramatic time and if we may assume that it was in fact early in the afternoon of the year 414 B.C. that these lines were first delivered on a stage and before an audience. In advancing this suggestion I am not ignoring the obvious fact that there need be no coincidence of true time and dramatic time in Greek drama. The *Clouds* of Aristophanes was first produced at the City Dionysia of 423 B.C., and was the fifth play to be performed in the Theatre of Dionysus on the day of its original production: this comedy, nevertheless, opens with Strepsiades pulling himself together after a sleepless night. The *Agamemnon*, like Euripides' *Iphigenia in Aulis*, opens before day has broken, while in the *Rhesus* we have to wait until verses 527ff. before the chorus welcomes the approach of dawn. The Greek dramatist was capable of creating an illusion of time even to the extent of suggesting it was the depth of night when the spectators were shading their eyes from the Mediterranean sun, but, for all that, it is tempting to believe that it actually was a little after mid-day when Prometheus asked his question and received so precise a reply.

Greek plays are short, in fact embarrassingly short for the modern producer. Their brevity is one of the reasons why Euripides was responsible for twenty-two productions or a total of eighty-eight plays and why Aeschylus is reputed to have written ninety plays. There were other reasons as well: the fact that their plays exploited traditional material and followed a set pattern in details as much as in structure facilitated speed of composition. But there are limits within which the dramatist, however adroit, must compose, and so the great tragedians seldom wrote for the Lenaea, whereas their comic counterparts wrote indifferently for the Lenaea and the City Dionysia. Still, the output of the Greek tragedians was staggering and has yet to be rivalled by the authors of the profusion of dramatic entertainment now being offered on the various television channels. Only one comparison suggests itself when it comes to the cracking pace at which Aeschylus, Sophocles and Euripides wrote for the stage, a comparison with the Elizabethan playwrights. Alfred Hart has established that the normal length of an Elizabethan play was 2500 lines. Documentary evidence, confirmed by the statements of the dramatists themselves—for example,

Shakespeare's 'two hours' traffic of our stage' in the Prologue of *Romeo and Juliet*—proves that two hours was the span of time allocated for the performance of the Elizabethan play.[13] Hart argues that a play of 2500 lines would have been performed in a few minutes in excess of two hours. Basing his claim on practical experiment, he maintains that blank verse from any play of the period can be read aloud clearly at the rate of twenty-two lines per minute, or 1320 lines per hour. But such a calculation allows nothing for pause to draw breath or for activity of any kind on the stage and, since plays were acted and not continuously read, Hart concludes that 2640 lines in two hours of reading should be reduced to 2300 lines when acted. Such a figure, if all else were equal, implies that my own estimate of 6500 or 7000 verses as the total number of lines delivered on one day of the City Dionysia represents some six hours of performance on the stage, and this assessment of time, even when we make a lavish allowance for short breaks between the individual plays, takes us an appreciable way from the idea of continuous performance stretching from dawn to dusk. If the five plays could be performed in six and not in ten or twelve hours, longer plays might clearly have been accommodated in the programme of the City Dionysia; and if no Greek play approaches anything like 2000 verses in length, it is not because insufficient time for performance was available. The type of drama we associate with fifth-century Athens did not permit a more extensive treatment. The plays were as long as they needed to be and additions would merely serve to destroy their essential character.

Hart carried out practical experiments. Experiments to determine the speed at which the *Iliad* may have been recited have been reported, but such experiments are of questionable value: readers are inexperienced and their mother-tongue not Greek; they read from a text and do not recite from memory; the experiments are of necessity contrived and it cannot be expected that the atmosphere and setting of an original performance may be reproduced. I know of no controlled experiment to ascertain the speed at which the metres of Greek drama were delivered, and I doubt the validity of a personal trial, especially if the experiment were conducted in a non-theatrical context. The longest play by Aeschylus to survive, the *Agamemnon*, includes the longest single choral ode in extant Greek drama, and how can a modern allow for the music and dancing which formed an integral part of the performance of a chorus? But the evidence offered by the Greek production at Epidaurus of Menander's *Dyskolos*, which was mentioned at the outset of this chapter, is more than a little startling, and appears to strengthen the opinion that very little more than six hours was sufficient to permit the staging of three tragedies, one satyr play and one comedy and to accommodate the intervals separating the plays. There would be no pressure of time, and everything, ceremonies and dramatic entertainment, might be comfortably included in a day's programme of events. I believe that the Athenians left the Theatre of Dionysus much earlier in the afternoon than has been suspected previously, and that when they left, they were not conscious of having been hurried through the events of a day strained to the point of breaking.

NOTES

1 See the remarks passed in the discussion which followed the paper by E. W. Handley in *Ménandre* (Entretiens sur l'Antiquité classique XVI, Geneva, 1970), pp. 35ff.

2 B. Hunningher, *Acoustics and Acting in the Theatre of Dionysus Eleuthereus* (Amsterdam, 1956), p. 21.

3 See É. Delebecque in *Classical Values and the Modern World* (Georges P. Vanier Memorial Lectures 1970–71, Ottawa, 1972), pp. 81ff.

4 A. E. Haigh, *The Attic Theatre* (Oxford,[3] 1907), p. 341.

5 In their revised edition of A. Pickard-Cambridge, *The Dramatic Festivals of Athens* (Oxford,[2] 1968), p. 272. Compare also N. C. Hourmouziades, *Production and Imagination in Euripides* (Athens, 1965), p. 6: 'According to the natural conditions of Attica at the end of March, performances could not possibly start earlier than eight o'clock in the morning or go on after six o'clock in the evening. Thus a period of *only* (my own italics) about ten hours seems to have been available.' It will become apparent that, in my opinion, six hours of performance on the stage would have been quite sufficient.

6 Aeschines, *Ctesiph.* 76 and Demosthenes, *Meid.* 74.

7 *Oeconomicus* iii. 7.

8 Haigh, op. cit. pp. 68–69; cf. Gould and Lewis, op. cit. pp. 58–59 and 67.

9 A. E. Raubitschek, *Transactions of the American Philological Association* 72 (1941), pp. 356–62.

10 See M. Werre-de Haas, *Aeschylus' Dictyulci* (Leiden, 1961), pp. 73–74.

11 Gould and Lewis, op. cit. pp. 64–65.

12 H. C. Baldry, *The Greek Tragic Theatre* (London, 1971), pp. 27–28.

13 Alfred Hart, *Shakespeare and the Homilies* (Melbourne, 1934), pp. 77ff. and 96ff.

The Spoken Word

In reducing 2640 lines in two hours of reading to 2300 lines in two hours of acting, Hart acquaints us with his views on the technique of Elizabethan acting: the Elizabethans, he says, 'were the best actors of their time; and good acting on their stage must have meant precisely the same as it has always meant on every other stage in every century, plenty of bustling action and vigorous elocution rather than unbroken monotony of continuous speech'.[1] Obviously, the more action the more time is needed to complete the performance of a play, but, according to Hart, no concession which will allow a reduction of playing time is to be made when the question of style of acting is raised. A solitary concession is permitted by this scholar, who admits the possibility that the Elizabethan actor may have spoken 'a little more rapidly' than his modern equivalent, the central position of the stage in the sixteenth-century theatre being cited as the factor which made a greater rapidity of speech possible.[2] Certainly the acoustic qualities of an open-air theatre, whether an Elizabethan public theatre or the Greek kind, will encourage speed of delivery, but a belief in an enhanced speed of speech seems interesting but hardly more than that, especially when we have so little evidence which relates to the speed at which ancient Greek was spoken and our scanty evidence is inconclusive.[3] The suggestion, nevertheless, assumes a crucial importance once its further implication is grasped, and grasped for the Greeks as well as for the Elizabethans. A clue is provided by Joseph when he endorses the arguments of Hart: 'I can easily believe that Shakespeare's company acted *Romeo and Juliet* in two hours, or very little more. I have directed amateurs in an uncut version of the play on an "Elizabethan-type" stage, and they rarely exceeded two hours and ten minutes and never took longer than two hours and a quarter. Their acting, of course, was not good; but their speaking was clear and could not only be understood, but communicated to the audience an experience of the imagery. It seems to me that Elizabethan actors were able to perform more swiftly than modern actors and to communicate much more completely, not only because their audience was more accustomed to listening, but because of their own training and abilities as actors.'[4] But the training undergone by modern actors is rigorous and their competence not to be slighted; the really significant comment passed by Joseph, I suggest, comes just before the end when we are told that 'their audience was more accustomed to listening', for it must be recognized that an actor's speed of delivery depends upon more than that actor's vocal powers, whether those powers be innate or the result of training; speed of delivery also depends upon, in fact is largely determined by, the pace at which an audience is able to understand and to absorb what is being said on the stage, and such a capacity to absorb is related not to degree of intelligence but to conditioning and habit. The collective ear of any group of spectators must be so attuned that speed of comprehension matches speed of delivery or else the actor on the stage is simply gabbling. A speed of delivery which renders an actor's words gabble for us may not have reduced speech to gabble for the Greeks and for the Elizabethans; indeed I am convinced that it was far from so doing.

My interest in this question was initially prompted by two remarks made by W. C. Greene some twenty years ago in an article entitled 'The spoken and the written word':[5] 'Greek drama was composed for the theatre and not for readers; it was intended to be seen and heard and felt instantly by an audience with many common bonds of experience and with the psychological reactions of groups seated together and not of isolated readers pondering at leisure' (p. 37), and '*Hamlet*, though written for the actors, and later printed, was composed for the stage, for oral presentation, and only incidentally for readers' (p. 30). The first of these statements posed a question: To what extent did the attitude of mind of the original spectators affect the form assumed by Greek drama? Greene's second comment aimed my question in a particular direction: How did 'oral presentation' affect the composition and production of Greek drama? The second comment also suggested a possible line of inquiry: perhaps the work of scholars whose immediate concern was the study of Elizabethan drama might be of some relevance to those primarily interested in the ancient theatre. Both sets of investigators meet similar problems, such as the problem of the double burial in Sophocles' *Antigone* and of Emilia and the handkerchief in *Othello*, and similar approaches should be applicable. I like to think that what was likely proved to be true, but its truth was established only after further consideration, and this consideration was inspired in its turn by the argument of E. A. Havelock that Greek culture was essentially oral in character before the fourth century B.C.,[6] and by the feeling of unease I experienced when, sitting in the theatre, I saw modern productions of plays first performed considerably more than two millennia ago.

Gilbert Murray claimed that 'one of our first difficulties in dealing with ancient literature is escape from the imaginative domination of the printed book'.[7] A specialist in English studies has spoken of 'the tyranny, the drugging influence, of print'.[8] While we today, of course, still communicate with each other by speech, the written, or to be more precise, the printed word has tended to oust the spoken word in contemporary society, although the balance is now being redressed because of the influence of two characteristically twentieth-century media, radio and television. In general, however, we have sacrificed much of our ability to listen with patience. A sermon, for instance, of more than fifteen minutes' duration taxes our good manners, whereas a century ago, and even more recently in rural districts, a diatribe whose orator thundered for a couple of hours was tolerated and apparently enjoyed. Yet, if we recall the Central American politician who harangues his supporters throughout a day and beyond, it will be appreciated that over a wide expanse of the globe oral communication has retained the hold it exercised in classical Greece and sixteenth-century England. Of greater significance than the actual ability to read and write is the attitude of mind displayed by the Athenians of the fifth century B.C. The evidence for literacy in the Athenian democracy has been collected by Harvey, who, under the heading 'some general considerations' remarks: 'Yet although the book was not a great rarity, it was none the less something out of the way, and it remains true that Greek culture was much more a culture of the spoken word than of the written word' (p. 588).[9] We should ask not to what extent could the Athenians read, but rather to what extent did they really read or, better still, to what extent did they read *for pleasure*. If we are thinking particularly of the theatre and the average citizen of Athens, the answer has already been given: 'If he cared about literature or music at all, he took them in through the ears, and in concentrated doses such as would stagger even the most persistent seeker after culture at the Edinburgh festival to-day.'[10]

I do not wish to deny that pure spectacle has a part to play in the theatre, though I would range myself on the side of Aristotle in affording it a low status as something falling within the province of the producer rather than within that of the dramatic poet (cf. *Poetics* 1450b 16–20). Nevertheless, in a society where the spoken word reigns supreme ears will replace eyes as the means, beyond all others, by which the artist has to communicate. To use the vocabulary of Marshall McLuhan, the Greeks lived in an 'ear world', whereas our world is that of the eyes. The ear world, moreover, is 'hot' but the eye world relatively cool and neutral.[11] The spoken word requires a personal confrontation and produces a sense of immediate involvement, for there must be a minimum of two persons engaged in any conversation. But a book demands just a single reader, and indeed it cannot accommodate more than the one reader at a time; the role of the book is passive—no book can answer back and it may be slammed shut and thus its contents avoided. Try getting rid of some of those who accost you in the street or indoors! You read a book from cover to cover and it comprises a unity whose argument ought to be progressive and coldly logical. Conversation flows, now forward, now backward, the spoken word being dynamic unlike the written or printed word, which is static and fixed for all time. But all this has been said before, indeed was said in antiquity by Socrates in the Platonic dialogue the *Phaedrus*. There Socrates can compare writing and painting, for a painted figure stands as if it were a living creature, but if a question is put to it, it may give no answer. So too it is impossible to examine written words, for they say only one and the same thing. The legitimate brother of the written word is the living and breathing word of the man who knows, and such a one will not resort to writing, a means of expression which is incapable of defending itself in argument and incapable of teaching the truth adequately. Personal inspiration is denied the student whose authority is a written text (*Phaedrus* 275d–277a).

Plato founded the Academy and Aristotle the Lyceum, and both institutes of higher education shared much in common. But there were also differences, as there were differences, of course, in the respective systems of philosophy. These differences, furthermore, mark a shift in emphasis from reliance on the spoken word to a growing reliance on the written word. We associate Aristotle with the systematic organization and classification of knowledge, and one symptom of this is the massive output of written material from the Lyceum, and these writings are very different in character and in style from the highly dramatic dialogue form favoured by Plato. Plato composed dialogues but Aristotle compiled 'collections' devoid of any literary pretensions.[12] Emphasis may change among philosophers, but the continuing supremacy of the spoken word throughout antiquity is revealed by the fact that, although we are wrong to assert that silent reading was extremely rare in the ancient world, books were normally read aloud by the Greeks and Romans.[13] Any generalization runs the risk of being thought rash, and I must not succumb to the temptation of drawing too sharp a distinction between our modern distrust of language and its total acceptance by Greeks and Elizabethans, and especially by Euripides and Shakespeare. Both playwrights were aware of the limitations of language, and both have been seen by literary critics to exploit the 'speech versus silence' theme and to acknowledge the inadequacy of mere words.[14] Yet an appreciation of the inadequacies of language simply serves to stress the commanding function of the spoken word in the societies in which Euripides and Shakespeare lived and worked.

Practice is reputed to make perfect: the ability to concentrate on the spoken word and to appreciate fully the force of what is being said, even when it is delivered more speedily than English is today, was nurtured at Athens not by special factors but by the basic character of ancient society and culture. The Greek theatre was acoustically superb and clarity of voice (witness that notorious joke cracked by Aristophanes in the *Frogs*, 303–4 at the expense of the unfortunate Hegelochus) the quality demanded from an actor because of the emphasis laid on the spoken word and not vice versa. We may compare the audience sitting in the Theatre of Dionysus and the audience attending a modern recital: a knowledge of the technicalities of music is not an essential prerequisite for the appreciation of a concert performance. According to Cicero, an ignorance of the rules of prosody did not prevent the ancient audience from reacting violently if verses were not delivered with an absolute precision: 'Where poetry is concerned the entire theatre roars out in the event of a false quantity, though the throng knows nothing about feet or rhythm, and does not realize why or how what upsets it does upset it. And yet nature itself has implanted in our ears an ability to judge every long and short sound as well as high and low tones' (*Orator* 173; cf. also *de Oratore* iii. 195–96). Technical knowledge, then, was replaced by a sensibility instinctively acquired, 'nature itself' (*ipsa natura*) being the source of instruction.

Living in a highly literate society, we find it difficult to appreciate how onerous a task it is to learn the art of reading and writing. Constant repetition is the basis of modern techniques by which a child is taught to read. If we can nearly all read today, it is the result of the combined weight of social and economic pressures: not to be able to read is to be branded as totally ignorant and one's chances of a stimulating (and lucrative) career are sadly diminished. It is the single reader, as we remarked before, who peruses a book, and this exercise requires some degree of privacy; artificial lighting means that one may read until late into the night. The simple type of life led by the ancients, their small and cramped houses, and the need, in the main, to confine their activities to the hours of daylight, all these factors militate against the encouragement of reading as a way of passing the time. But as much promoted the influence of the spoken word as restricted the wide-spread use of the written word. Fifth-century Athens was a democracy where every issue was discussed and debated by the male citizens in the assembly. We are obliged to read parliamentary reports, but the Athenian might well be in the assembly himself, listening to the various arguments in favour of or opposed to the adoption of a particular policy. Again, few ages have been so obsessed with litigation as fifth-century Athens and sixteenth-century England. In the Greek court of law the litigant presented his own case, but might, from the late fifth century, employ a speech writer or *logographos* to write a speech for him, and the competent *logographos* would compose a speech suited to the personality as well as to the cirumstances of the speaker. The *logographos* is the legal equivalent of the playwright, while the litigant, who would learn the speech composed for him by heart and then deliver it before the jury, corresponds to the actor. The jury, large in number and representative of all the citizens in its membership, was like the audience attending the dramatic festivals. In short, what was presented on the stage was far from being alien to the actual experience of life enjoyed by the average Athenian, and in a life which climatic conditions encouraged one to spend out-of-doors, in the assembly and in the law-court, as in the theatre, the spoken word was unchallenged and had no rival.

In a court an advocate must explain the facts of a case, or, at least, his side's version of the facts. Contemporary dramatists tend to fight shy of inflicting upon an audience speeches of a length common in Greek and Elizabethan plays. More than length of speech has been modified, for contents have also been changed; the contemporary dramatist does not write the type of expository speech, stating the case for and against, so frequently to be found in the Greek tragedians or Shakespeare. To quote characteristic examples from the first and the last of the Greek tragedians whose plays have survived might possibly be thought unfair on the grounds that Aeschylus is 'unsophisticated' and Euripides too much of an innovator. But if we turn to the latest play by Sophocles, in the *Oedipus Coloneus* we come across first Oedipus' self-defence with its plea of diminished responsibility (verses 960ff.) and, then, the (by our standards) excessively long speech in which Polyneices explains the reason for his appearance before his parent (verses 1284ff.). We regard the long expository speech as a dramatically crude device and so it is banished from our stage, but it is the words which count in the Greek and in the Elizabethan theatre, both audiences being entranced by word-play and word-pattern to the extent, for example, of warmly welcoming the pun, a form of humour which is apt to fall very flat today, and both peoples sharing a passion for litigation which is reflected by both the expository speech and debate between the characters presented on the stage.

We read in the *Orestes* of Euripides that 'a long speech is better than a short one and clearer to hear' (verses 640–41), and this comment is to be taken as a typically Greek remark. Brevity is no merit when the spoken word is supreme. The consequences which flow from a realization of the primacy of the spoken word are as crucial to our understanding of Greek drama as they are also numerous. Violence, as we are told, does not occur on the Greek stage. Too often it is assumed that such a convention marks the ancient producer's inability to create in view of the spectators a convincing impression of violent action. Yet this assumption imposes an arbitrary standard of realism on Greek drama, something which we have no right and no reason to demand. The case of the chorus proves that so-called conventions may be formed for other reasons quite apart from convenience; conventions may be derived from tradition and we look to the possible origins of drama among the Greeks to explain the presence of a chorus in a Greek play. If it can be suggested that the convention which banished violence from the Greek stage is a convention dictated by tradition, and if it can further be shown that the convention was not rigidly observed, then we must reckon with the possibility that the Greek dramatist *chose quite deliberately* not to depict violence, preferring to have acts of violence reported by a messenger. If the playwright made a conscious choice, and was not compelled by the physical limitations of his theatre to exclude acts of violence, it follows that a report of violence was considered to be dramatically more effective than violence itself on stage, and we must proceed by asking why this was so. The answer to this question, I suggest, is provided by the oral character of Greek society in the fifth century B.C. and a consequent preference for the spoken word. But we are now beginning to anticipate conclusions whose foundations will only be secured if we first investigate the possible origin of the convention and then look to see if the convention was as universally observed as is often implied.

What do we mean by 'violence' when we use this word of the Greek theatre? Surely we mean death, though death may be peaceful as well as violent and plenty of other events apart from the act of dying qualify or may qualify as violent. By Greek standards the abduction of women is a heinous crime and one invariably accompanied by some measure of force. But let us accept that the occurrence of violence is not something which we read back into Greek drama and that death represents the ultimate on any scale of violence. Arnott believes that the practicalities of stage production explain the apparent reluctance by the Greeks to depict death on the stage itself: it is awkward to remove a dead body from the stage or for any actor to be on the stage feigning death for some length of time; the dramatist, moreover, could not afford to have one of his three speaking actors immobilized and therefore unable to take a further part in the play.[15] If a character does not actually die, other difficulties can arise—if Oedipus wears a different mask after tearing out his own eyes, he should blind himself off-stage in order to avoid the embarrassment of changing into an appropriately bloody mask in front of the audience. These, it is true, are problems, and, unless we are prepared to revive an old argument and to claim that it was religious tabu which prevented blood being shed on stage, it seems difficult to identify a traditional element which will serve as a convincing alternative to the theory that the physical limitations of theatre and production determined the convention. Yet I would remind the reader of a significant conjunction of dates, *circa* 550 B.C. for the institution of contests among rhapsodes reciting from the Homeric poems at the Panathenaic festival and 534 B.C. for the first tragic productions at the City Dionysia by Thespis. This brief, yet not too brief, interval of time adds credibility to the suggestion that it was the performances of rhapsodes, professional reciters of the Homeric poems, which led to the addition of a dramatic ingredient and so caused songs by a chorus to develop into true drama. Thus Else comments: 'The rhapsodes did not merely recite Homer, they acted him, and from this quasi-impersonation of Homeric characters it was only a step to full impersonation, from the rhapsode who momentarily spoke in the person of Achilles or Odysseus to the "actor" who presented himself as Achilles or Odysseus.'[16] The Homeric poems represent a mixture of narrative description and dramatic speech (see our p. 51), and, if there is in fact some connection in origin between recitation from Homer and Greek tragic drama, the former having influenced and even helped to inspire the latter, a preference for narrative description rather than for action on the stage may be referred to the first beginnings of Greek drama and explained as a convention derived from traditon and not as something forced on an unwilling playwright.

Death may certainly occur before the eyes of a Greek audience, though the argument that the expression of Aristotle which Hubbard translates as 'on stage' (*en toi phaneroi*), a phrase which appears when the philosopher, in defining *pathos* as an element of plot, mentions death, clearly does mean 'on stage' fails to carry conviction (*Poetics* 1452b 12).[17] Euripides' Alcestis and Hippolytus do die on stage, though the first death, however untimely, is hardly violent and Hippolytus' life ebbs away, the real damage having been done already off-stage. A reference by Cicero shows that in Sophocles' *Odysseus Acanthoplex* the mortally wounded hero was brought on stage (*Tusc.* ii. 49–50), as, of course, was Heracles in the *Trachiniae*. In the *Rhesus* the charioteer of Rhesus comes on stage to report his master's death; he is himself grievously wounded (cf. verses 793ff.) and claims to be no longer able to stand on his feet, though the extent of his injury does not prevent him from arguing hotly with Hector. Acts of general violence also occur in the sight of the audience, and surprisingly often when we allow for the few plays to have survived, e.g. only seven of Aeschylus' reputed ninety plays. Women and children may be threatened with abduction, as the daughters of Danaos are in the *Supplices* of Aeschylus (verses 903ff.) and the sons of Heracles in Euripides' *Heraclidae* (verses 55ff.). In the latter play, when an attempt is actually made (verses 269ff.), Demophon threatens to strike Copreus and is urged to restraint by the chorus (verses 271 and 273). The sons of Heracles take refuge at an altar and this type of scene is favoured by Euripides: the heroine of the *Andromache* seeks safety in the shrine of Thetis (verses 42–44), while an altar protects Creusa from the wrath of her son in the *Ion* (verses 1250ff.); it is possible that Paris in the *Alexander* also found sanctuary at an altar.[18] In Euripides' *Phoenissae* Creon orders Antigone to be dragged from the body of the dead Polyneices (verses 1660–61), and Sophocles' Creon in the *Oedipus Coloneus*, having seized Ismene off-stage, removes her sister

Antigone from the stage itself despite the vigorous intervention of the chorus (verses 818ff.): 'Forcibly (*pros bian*) do I go' (verse 845), Antigone cries as she is taken away. The following part of this tragedy is remarkable for its lack of a messenger-type speech. Theseus rescues the girls and they all rejoin Oedipus on the stage (verses 1096ff.). In answer to his request that he be told of what happened, Antigone informs her father that he must listen to Theseus (verses 1115–18), and we are led to expect an account of the rescue from the king of Athens, but our expectation is disappointed; preferring deeds to words, Theseus leaves Oedipus' daughters to tell the story and hurries on to report the arrival of yet another mysterious stranger (verses 1139ff.). Sophocles springs a surprise upon us by not having the rescue described when we have been carefully prepared to expect an account, first from Antigone, the rescued, and then from Theseus, the rescuer, and one wonders whether the absence of a report is related to the earlier presence of violence on the stage, these being mutually exclusive alternatives. Violent behaviour of another kind is illustrated by the altercation between Menelaus and an old man who acts as his brother Agamemnon's messenger in the *Iphigenia in Aulis* (verses 304ff.). Menelaus seizes and reads a letter from Agamemnon which cancels an earlier instruction that Iphigenia be sent to Aulis. The pair struggle over the possession of the letter (verses 309ff.) and Menelaus threatens the old man with his staff. When Agamemnon arrives his servant can claim that the letter was wrestled from him by force (*biai* in verse 315), and Agamemnon himself repeats the expression, asking why Menelaus is handling the old man with force (*biai* in verse 319). Vocabulary as much as the sense of the passage suggests a fair measure of violent activity on stage (cf. verse 317 with its *thorubos* and *logon akosmia*).

It is true that Euripides has Heracles in the *Hercules Furens* and Medea in the *Medea* murder their children off-stage, but in his *Cresphontes* it seems that the dramatist portrayed on stage a mother on the point of slaying her own son with an axe, though this mother was unaware of the identity of her proposed victim. Instructive is the comment passed by Plutarch on the audience's reaction to this scene, for it refers to an audience brought to its feet in fear that violence will be perpetrated before a third party may intervene.[19] Other weapons may be deployed threateningly on the stage: the hero of Euripides' *Orestes* menaces first the Phrygian slave and later Hermione with his sword (cf. verses 1519, and 1575 and 1608), and Ion draws his bow against Xuthos in the *Ion* (verse 524). Earlier in the same play Ion uses his bow to drive away birds, and the critic Demetrius refers to the swan which is threatened by Ion, pointing out what scope for movement is offered by such action: the actor must snatch up his weapon and look upwards towards the offending bird.[20] In the *Philoctetes* of

Sophocles Philoctetes draws his bow against Odysseus (verse 1299) and the use of a bow on stage has a special interest, for the bow is particularly associated with certain characters. The bow is the chosen instrument of destruction wielded by Heracles and so used by him to murder his children in the *Hercules Furens* (verses 969–70); Apollo and Artemis are divinities with outstanding skill as archers, and it was presumably the bow which was employed by Artemis in Sophocles' *Niobe*, a play in which, if we may trust the evidence of a papyrus fragment, at least one of the daughters of Niobe was struck down on stage.[21] Even more spectacular and similarly enacted in view of the spectators, is the suicide of Evadne in the *Supplices* of Euripides: the bereaved wife stands on a rock like a bird on its perch, and from there she dashes herself down onto the funeral pyre of her husband Capaneus (verses 1014ff.). A parallel to this setting is provided in the *Philoctetes*, when Philoctetes threatens to throw himself to the ground (verses 1000ff.), and, if it is thought that the Sophoclean scene may be accommodated on the Greek stage, there can be no real objection to our also accepting Evadne's leap to death; this need not demand more than a slight drop, since we should not seek the kind of difference in levels necessary to make the effect of the leap realistic. We must avoid the trap of being excessively realistic, a trap which has recently ensnared Anthony Burgess in his translation and adaption of the *Oedipus Tyrannus*.[22] Burgess meddles with the Greek text to the extent of having Oedipus blind himself before the spectators. Having pierced his own eyes, Oedipus in this version of Sophocles' play delivers a solitary pair of lines. Why? 'Men whose eyes have just been put out do not, unless they are still under a local anaesthetic, talk reasonably or even unreasonably: they do not talk at all,' writes Burgess, and, for all its sarcasm, what he says is true when applied to real life and real people, but neither Evadne nor Oedipus are living persons in that sense; they are characters in plays and nothing more.

We are not compelled to assume that the actor playing the role of Evadne actually jumped from the roof of a stage-building to the stage below, for the often quoted parallel offered by the 'leap' of the Phrygian slave in the *Orestes* is very suspect. It is assumed that the Phrygian does jump from the roof of the stage-building onto the stage, no slight drop, for he tells the chorus that he escaped the slaughter inside over the cedar beams that roof the porch and through the Doric triglyphs (verses 1369ff.). Yet his arrival on stage is announced by the chorus which refers to the usual sound of the opening door (verses 1366–68; cf. *Ion*, 515–16 and *Helen*, 859–60). Too often we are happy to accept the opinion of the scholiast when he claims that these verses were inserted to avoid an actor having to leap down onto the stage, an example, in other words, of an actor's interpolation into the original text. But this apparent difficulty may be eliminated

in one of several ways. It has, for instance, been suggested that this character 'is of course describing the inner courtyard scene when he scrambled
out of the women's quarters before reaching the visible outer doors which
he has just walked through in the ordinary way'.[23] If such an interpretation
of the lines is considered to be too subtle, we can fall back on the argument that the slave lowered himself down from the roof and did not jump.
But why accept the slave's statement at face value? The Phrygian is an
emotional character and it would be a nice touch if he entered via the
central door of the stage-building, but, in a flood of fear and hyperbole,
talked of having clambered over the roof. This is what might well be
described as a 'comic' character, something to be taken into account as
well in any explanation of his mode of entry onto the stage.[24]

However it was staged, the death of Evadne is much more devastating
than those of Alcestis and Hippolytus. If action of such intensity could be
portrayed before the spectators and not merely reported by a messenger,
we must surely consider the likelihood that, the spoken word being preferred to visual effects, action was more readily appreciated and enjoyed
by the audience when that action was described rather than when that
action was seen to take place, and so we find the multitude of messenger
speeches in Greek tragedy. Well over a century ago an editor of Euripides
commenting on the messenger's speech and its news of calamity, noted
that 'the ear, but not the eye, was the chosen vehicle of pathos to the
Greeks'.[25] As an explanation of the convention, convenience is at the
best only part of the answer: what was convenient and what was traditional,
and also what was, by the standards of the ancients, more effective dramatically, all three factors taken together explain the popularity of speeches
delivered by a messenger. The Greek theatre is so huge that visual effects
have a restricted impact, but it is at the same time acoustically so magni-
ficent that, given clarity of expression, hearing is unimpeded. And this is
much more than simply saying that the ears were able to catch more than
the eyes could see. Physical sight was replaced by what was 'seen' by an
adroitly stimulated imagination, and the imagination was stimulated by
an actor's words. Set free from the need to allow for details of staging,
the dramatist may revel in what has been aptly called the 'grand guignol'
type of death.[26] The facts related by the messenger are enlivened by the
sheer horror of the deed committed and by a description laced with
lurid, melodramatic language. If the 'messenger' has suffered some
outrage himself, and that outrage was perpetrated in seemingly innocent
circumstances, the horror is that much more acute: thus in Euripides'
Hecuba Polymestor describes how he was blinded and his children
slaughtered by the Trojan captives while he sat at his ease in the midst of
these women (verses 1145ff.), and his present condition as he delivers

his message adds a further dimension to his words (cf. verses 1056ff.). Again our sense of horror may be reinforced by screams or cries for help off-stage or our nerves twisted by the startled reaction of members of the chorus (cf. *Agamemnon*, 1343ff.). The audience draws on the resources of its imagination to supplement the gaps in the narrative and thus is obliged to participate in the action of the play. The picture consequently conjured up in the mind is electrifying. We are each of us haunted by personal fears and fantasies, and no author can hope to sound the depths of the mind of every member of his audience and then to exploit these basic emotions. An impressionistic technique which drops hints and sketches broad outlines is the best means by which an audience may be persuaded to identify itself with the characters on the stage or, momentarily, off the stage. The noise of the scaffold being erected and the thud as the victim falls through the trap is more unsettling than actually seeing the execution oneself. A report of something which has occurred away from the view of the spectators telescopes the action of the drama, reducing the time required for its performance; it also serves to intensify the horror inherent in any act of aggression or self-mutilation. The report of violence may be more than just better drama, for it can even be more 'real' if the ears are the sense organ on which one relies, as our own expression 'seeing is believing' must give way to the expression 'hearing is believing' when the spoken word reigns supreme. If one believes, one can fully identify with the character portrayed by the actor, sympathy being so marked as to become empathy. That the Greek audience was capable of such identification is clearly shown by Plato in attacking dramatic poetry and by Aristotle in his defence of the same art. One of the several reasons which Plato advances for excluding poetry from his ideal state is the fact that we take pleasure in the sufferings of the hero presented to us by Homer or on the stage, and so are beguiled into suffering with the sufferer, thus undermining our own resolution when faced by a personal calamity (*Republic* 605c–606b). For Aristotle tragedy achieves *catharsis* through pity and fear (*Poetics* 1449b 27), and, however we interpret *catharsis*, the emotions of pity and fear must be understood as being excited in the spectator as a consequence of the action taking place on the stage.

The combination of the messenger's words and the spectator's imagination was more effective in the ancient theatre than physical action on the stage. In the *Helen* of Euripides one of the characters in the play, Teucer, can speak of having seen with his eyes and seeing with his mind (*nous* in verse 122). The Greek dramatists were not only aware of the power of the individual imagination, a force which enables one to 'see' in the present what had actually been seen in the past, but also featured it in

some of their works. In the *Agamemnon* Cassandra lets her imagination
run riot as she rehearses her own as well as Agamemnon's death to
provide the audience with a messenger-type speech delivered by one of
the victims of the violence and delivered in advance of the event itself
(verses 1072ff.); Cassandra sees the children of Thyestes as well, like the
shapes which appear to us in dreams (verses 1217–22), and this the chorus
can understand and fear (verses 1242–44). Another demented woman in
Aeschylus is the ill-fated Io, who raves, seeing her tormentor in her
imagination (*Prometheus Vinctus*, 561ff.). Towards the conclusion of
the *Choephori* Aeschylus depicts an Orestes who imagines himself beset
by Furies, intent on extracting revenge from a matricide: 'You do not
see them,' Orestes tells the chorus, 'but I see them' (verse 1061), and so
surely did the audience also. If we compare Orestes' description of the
Furies here and their actual appearance when they come into the theatre
in the final play of the *Oresteia* trilogy, it is possible to gauge the superiority
of imagination to reality when it comes to horrific description.[27] The
Furies, as imagined by Orestes in the *Choephori* are like Gorgons, wear
dark clothes and are thickly wreathed with snakes (verses 1048–50). The
last detail is gruesome, but worse has still to come—their eyes drip blood
(verse 1058). The description of the Furies in the *Eumenides* is toned
down, for the absolutely terrifying details, the snakes and blood, are
missing. The Furies may have a taste for blood (cf. verses 183–84), but
now their eyes no longer drip blood but ooze rheum (verse 54), and this
change from blood to something much less arresting typifies the limitations associated with what is seen by the eyes as opposed to what is
imagined in the mind. The Furies, according to the *Eumenides*, are otherwise women, but not women, Gorgons, but not Gorgons, featherless
(presumably they are winged), dark, wear clothes unfit to be brought before
gods and men, and are like old women and aged children (verses 47–48,
48–49, 51, 52, 55–56, 69 and 69), a strange mixture of features which has
suggested to one critic they are to be thought of as bats. It would seem,
however, that the Furies are like no creature known to gods and men
(cf. verses 410–12). Their faces (verse 990), indeed their whole appearance
is terrifying enough to add credibility to the tradition that their arrival in
the theatre caused the young to faint and women to miscarry, but still,
for all that, the Furies of the *Eumenides*, stripped of their snakes and eyes
dripping blood, in terms of sheer horror, do not measure up to the Furies
described by the agonized Orestes.

The exploitation of the imaginative powers of the audience was too
attractive a technique to be ignored by Euripides. The dying Alcestis sees
Charon's boat (verses 252ff.), and, feeling herself being led into the realm
of the dead, asks 'do you not see?' (verse 259). In the *Bacchae* Pentheus

cannot see the god who stands at the side of the captive Dionysus (verses 501–2), but later seems to see two suns and two versions of the city of Thebes and Dionysus now transformed into a bull (verses 918–22). But the best examples to be found in the plays of the younger dramatist are offered by his handling of the story of Orestes. In the play of the same name Orestes 'sees' the Furies again (verses 253ff.; note especially verses 259 and 272; cf. also verse 408), but Euripides must embroider the Aeschylean situation, and so Electra, when she tries to check her brother's convulsions, is thought herself to be one of the Furies, and Orestes draws his bow (see above) in an attempt to ward off his imaginary adversaries (verses 268ff.). But to find an Orestes whose reaction to his own hallucinations is even more violent, it is necessary to look at the *Iphigenia in Tauris* and the report which Iphigenia receives from the herdsman (verses 281ff.) The herdsman and his companions have spotted a pair of strangers—Orestes and Pylades, of course—one of whom is seized by a fit of madness, shaking his head up and down and trembling to the tips of his fingers. The deranged man cries out, for he sees the Furies keen for his death. Snakes, breath of fire, even the dead Clytemnestra in the arms of one of the Furies, who wings her way to on high in order to cast the body down, are imagined by Orestes, though what he really sees are cattle and dogs. His frenzy is such that Orestes falls upon the herd, sword in hand (cf. the description of Heracles in *Hercules Furens*, 922ff.), striking indiscriminately at the animals in a mistaken belief that they are the Furies, until the sea foams with blood. Foam also disfigures Orestes' chin as madness leaves him and he falls to the ground. What this passage loses from being a description of the ravings of Orestes and not featuring the son of Agamemnon on the stage himself, it more than makes up by the savagery of the action so vividly related by the herdsman, thus confirming the opinion that the imagination offers the playwright more scope than is allowed by the visual.

Convention is not to be equated with limitation, as Euripides shows us time and time again as in messenger speech after messenger speech he deploys every conceivable trick of the dramatist. Each report by a messenger has its own particular quality and here I must be content to refer very briefly to only three, one from the *Bacchae*, one from the *Ion*, and a further example from the *Iphigenia in Tauris*. The report of Pentheus' arrival among the Bacchae (verses 1043ff.) includes an idyllic setting, which in its very innocence underlines the horror of the violence soon to be perpetrated there, a 'miracle', the voice of god, a blaze of divine light, women gripped in a passion inspired by Dionysus, and the appalling death of Pentheus with his own mother leading the pack of frenzied devotees. For pure melodrama one may turn to the *Ion* with its description of Creusa's attempt to murder the son she has yet to recognize (verses 1122ff.). The report is long and the scene set in elaborate detail; its climax comes when a bird laps up the poisoned wine poured away on the ground by Ion and then dies, and dies in a fashion which can only be called devastating (verses 1196–1208). The *Iphigenia in Tauris* includes an account of the attempt made by Orestes and his sister to flee the land of the Tauri (verses 1327ff.) which is remarkable for its ups and downs, and which ends with the escape still to be effected.

It is a cardinal principle that convention must not be thought limitation, and this principle also applied to the restricted number of speaking actors allowed a Greek tragedian. Even when the use of a third speaking actor had been firmly established in the second half of the fifth century B.C., debate on the stage between just two actors is the general rule; when three actors appear in the same scene, it is usually only two of the three who converse together at a particular point in the scene. Thus in Sophocles' *Antigone* Creon, Antigone and Ismene meet together on the stage (verses 526ff.). After what are very much introductory words from Creon (verses 531–35), the ruler falls silent while the two sisters converse (verses 536–60); then Creon intervenes (verses 561–62) and he and Ismene proceed to exchange words until the end of the scene (verses 563ff.). The attribution by critics of verse 572, 'O dearest Haemon, how your father dishonours you', to Antigone, an attribution which ignores the evidence of our manuscripts which assign the line to Ismene, seems to me to represent a desperate attempt to give Antigone at least something to say, and I would also hesitate long before accepting the chorus as the speaker of verse 574. Again in the *Helen* of Euripides Theoclymenus encounters Helen and they speak together at length (verses 1186ff.). The disguised Menelaus is present on the stage as well and his presence is noticed (verse 1203), but he says his first words considerably later (verse 1251) and, when he does, the conversation continues between Theoclymenus and Menelaus and now it is Helen who is ignored. It is merely at the conclusion of the scene that she is allowed to speak (verses 1294–1300), and these words simply mark that the scene has reached its end. The wealth of characters we associate with a play by Shakespeare suggests a very different technique, but appearances can notoriously be deceptive and the true position somewhat surprising: 'Most scenes in Shakespeare's plays involve less than five active players on stage at one time. Even where there are a large number of actors on stage, the action is confined to a scene between two or three . . . The actor generally had to play with one or two others.'[28]

Greek drama does not develop in the same way as vegetable life evolves, even though Aristotle tells us that tragedy 'stopped altering' when it had reached its 'full growth' (*Poetics* 1449a 14–15). It is tempting, of course, to argue as if drama were something organic, but then we ignore the warning issued by the redating of Aeschylus' *Supplices*, a play long considered our earliest extant tragedy because of the dominant role of the chorus in the play. But we are wrong to think in terms of a chorus which declines in importance from the height achieved in the *Supplices* until, in the fourth century, it is entirely eliminated.[29] Three actors are not necessarily better than two, and, if the tragedian never went beyond the employment of three speaking actors in a play, it was primarily not for 'economic' reasons but because he felt no need for a further performer. The failure to feel such a need is the more remarkable when we take into account the greater number of speaking characters who appear in the latest plays, in the *Orestes* Electra, Helen, Hermione, Orestes, Menelaus, Tyndareus, Pylades, the Messenger, the Phrygian and Apollo, and in the *Phoenissae* Jocasta, the Paidagogos, Antigone, Polyneices, Eteocles, Creon, Menoeceus, Teiresias, the two Messengers and Oedipus. When he refers to this restriction on the number of actors, Haigh made a comment worth remembering: 'The dialogue gained in clearness and simplicity, owing to the fewness of the persons taking part in it.'[30] We must think of two, or at the most three, actors speaking formalized language, for after all what they speak is in verse, and arranged in formalized grouping on the stage of a theatre so large that some point of visual focus on which the audience might concentrate is highly desirable. What is being said is all important; our attention must be seized and held by the intensity of the debate which is being carried on, and this is a debate designed to score points rather than to reproduce the character of authentic conversation, something which is in any case impossible with only two participants. The debate, however, was not divorced from an experience of true life: echoes of the assembly and the law-courts may be detected, and one surviving play, Aeschylus' *Eumenides*, is in fact set, for the most part, in an existing court of law, the Areopagus of Athens. The arguments before the Areopagus advanced by both sides are more clever than convincing: the Furies can quote the example offered by Zeus, who imprisoned his own father Cronos (verses 640–42), to counter Apollo's claim that the murder of Clytemnestra was not comparable to that of Agamemnon; when Apollo quotes Athene as a living proof of his argument that the only true parent is the father (verses 657ff.), he makes as blatant an appeal to the personal prejudice of a member of the jury as was ever made in an Athenian court, and his argument strikes home, for, in registering her vote, the goddess Athene comments on her lack of a mother and declares herself entirely on the side of the male (verses 736–40); Apollo, moreover, is not above reinforcing his case with an inducement in pointing out the advantages which will accrue to an Athens which saved Orestes (verses

667–73). We may imagine the excitement among the audience as the votes are cast and Orestes is acquitted by the skin of his teeth. The fact that everybody knew in advance what the verdict had to be means nothing; one need not be endowed with second-sight to be able to anticipate the outcome of almost any play or film today, but an ability to predict what will eventually transpire will not prevent the spectator from enjoying the skill with which the playwright brings about an outcome which, only too often, is inevitable. 'I must prove myself a clever speaker' is the kind of sentiment with which a character in a Greek play introduces his arguments (cf. *Medea*, 522), and it is by this process of proving himself or herself to be a clever speaker that the character ensures that the attention of the spectators is riveted to his words.

The language and the sentiments of the law-courts may colour a speech, whether or not a dramatist stages his play in a court-room. Thus, in defending himself against suspicion of having raped his step-mother, Phaedra, Hippolytus opens his reply to his father Theseus with a pair of clichés drawn from the law-court, the 'unaccustomed as I am to public speaking' platitude and a standard protest averring that it is necessity rather than choice which persuades him to offer a defence (*Hippolytus*, 986–87 and 990–91); before his speech is ended, Hippolytus can refer to his lack of a witness (verse 1022) and offer an oath by Zeus (verses 1025–26). The influence of procedure both in the law courts and in the assembly is to be seen in Euripides' *Orestes*. The arguments for and against the matricide are repeated, but the setting at first is not that of a trial, as Tyndareus, Menelaus and Orestes meet. Tyndareus shows no grain of sympathy for Orestes, going as far as to state that he ought to have taken legal action against his mother when Agamemnon was murdered (verses 491ff.), a suggestion as anachronistic as any may be. When he replies on his own behalf Orestes makes the first point of his defence a father's superior claim as parent (verses 552–56). A trial does follow, this time before the Argive assembly, but it occurs away from the spectators' view and is the subject of a messenger's speech (verses 866ff.). A speech from Orestes is reported (verses 932ff.), but this is preceded by a succession of speeches from two named and two unnamed individuals who clearly represent types familiar from the assembly: first we have the double-tongued Talthybius (verses 887ff.) and Diomedes, a man of few words (verses 898ff.), and then a 'ceaselessly babbling, mightily bold Argive who is no Argive' (verses 902ff.) and, to complete the second pair of opposites, an 'honest farmer' (verses 917ff.).

Perhaps the most gripping session in a modern court comes when witnesses and the accused are exposed to cross-examination in an attempt to elicit the truth. In an Athenian court of law a litigant was allowed to put specific questions to his opponent and the opponent was obliged to reply. A type of cross-examination is exploited most effectively by Sophocles in his *Trachiniae*. In the tragedy Lichas arrives at the royal home in advance of his master Heracles, bringing with him captive women. Lichas tells Deianeira that Heracles has destroyed a city and that these captives are spoils of victory. One of the women excites the interest and pity of the queen, but, when asked the identity of the woman, Lichas professes ignorance of this fact (verses 307ff.). Lichas and the women then leave the stage, and a messenger devastates Deianeira with a very different story; he claims that Lichas has previously declared, and declared in the presence of many witnesses, that Heracles destroyed the city because of his passion for the captive noticed by Deianeira, she being the daughter of the king: he further adds that Deianeira must not expect the woman simply to serve the household as a slave (verses 351ff.). Urged on by the chorus, Deianeira decides to force the truth from Lichas, and it is at this point in the play that Lichas, returning to the stage, is subjected to a cross-examination conducted by the messenger (verses 400ff.). Deianeira, however, opens with a direct question, asking who the woman is again, and, when Lichas again states that he does not know her parentage, the messenger resorts to a circuitous approach, forcing Lichas to acknowledge that he is addressing his mistress, the queen and wife of Heracles, and asking him to stipulate the punishment he deserves if found to be untrue to Deianeira. Lichas' attempt to slip away is forestalled, and the messenger presses on with more questions, reminding Lichas of his declaration before an abundance of witnesses. Lichas cannot deny the truth of this and has to fall back on an excuse which may be feeble but is certainly not rare in legal proceedings—I said this is what I heard, but it is not the same thing, to state an opinion and to present a positive fact (verses 425–26). But once more he fails to wriggle away, for he is now reminded that it was under oath that he said he was bringing a wife for Heracles, and all that is left to Lichas is an indignant question addressed to Deianeira as to who on earth this man is. A crisp enough answer follows immediately—the man who was present to hear you say that it was passion for the woman which brought about the destruction of the city (verses 431–33). Lichas can say nothing other than observe that the sane do not indulge in nonsensical chatter with the mad. The deadlock is resolved by a deceptively tolerant statement by Deianeira, which persuades Lichas, at long last, to admit the truth to the queen (verses 436ff.).

The Athenian penchant for linguistic subtleties and verbal pyrotechnics was only too evident if we may trust Cleon's speech to the assembly at the time of the Mytilene debate, for on that occasion the orator warned his fellow-countrymen against being seduced by fine language, condemned them for being 'spectators of speeches', and characterized them as 'slaves' of every new paradox (Thuc. iii. 38). It is such a claim that explains Antigone's surprising statement (and its justification) that she would not have persevered with her attempt to bury the dead if the body had not been that of a brother but that of one of her own children or husband, for she might secure another child or husband, something impossible in the case of a brother, both parents now being dead (*Antigone*, 905–12). Cleon concluded his words with the accusation that the Athenians were less like men deliberating on the affairs of state than they were like men sitting to listen to a sophist's display. The appearance in the second half of the fifth century B.C. of the sophists and the consequent development of the art of rhetoric had an impact which it is difficult to exaggerate. Cleon's words recall the performances put on by sophists such as Hippias and Gorgias at Olympia and at other great festivals, a type of competition previously associated with the poets. Of course, in the case of Euripides the influence of the sophists is marked: thus, in reply to Creon's herald in the *Supplices*, who argues in favour of monarchical government (verses 409ff.), Theseus begins his vindication of democracy (verses 426ff.) as if a sophist engaged in competition with a rival: 'since you provoked this contest (*agon*), listen, for you have proposed a contest (*hamilla*) of words' (verses 427–28).[31] The sophist Gorgias came to Athens in 427 B.C.; his writings included a rhetorical exercise entitled the *Helen*, in which the woman of that name defended herself against the charge that she must be held responsible for the Trojan War and the suffering it produced. Comparable is the debate in the *Trojan Women* of Euripides where again Helen attempts to justify herself and her deeds (verses 914ff.). This display of verbal ingenuities leads to the surprising conclusion that Helen has actually saved rather than destroyed Greece! Hecuba's answer (verses 969ff.), however, is its match, and it needed to be if it were to demolish the other woman's talent for persuasion (cf. verses 966–68). Yet neither address to Menelaus, who is cast in the role of arbitrator, carries conviction; both set-pieces make splendid theatre and that alone was the purpose of the playwright in including them in his play. One detail in Hecuba's speech is especially worthy of our attention: Helen has put much of the blame on the goddess Aphrodite; Hecuba retorts (verses 989–90) that every stupidity on the part of man constitutes Aphrodite and the goddess' name correctly begins *aphrosyne*, the Greek word which is the opposite of *sophrosyne* or the ability to control one's appetites, including the sexual urge. Such a play on words is not only absolutely characteristic of Greek drama, but also stresses the differences between our own and the ancient concept of dramatic entertainment, for false etymologies of this type are hardly likely to appeal to the audience in a modern theatre. It needs a culture dominated by the spoken word if such verbal tricks are to be appreciated. Certainly, the Greek tragedians, like Shakespeare, provide plenty of examples of punning on proper names: Aeschylus plays on the name of Polyneices, 'Much Strife', in his *Seven against Thebes* (verses 829–30), on the name Prometheus, 'Foresight', in the *Prometheus Vinctus* (verses 85–86), and on the names Helen and Apollo in the *Agamemnon* (verses 681ff. and 1085–86); Sophocles offers a similar example in the *Ajax* (verses 430–33), while further instances in Euripides include the *Ion*, verses 661–63, *Phoenissae*, verses 636–37 and 1493 (Polyneices again), and *Bacchae*, verses 507–8.

According to a fragment of Euripides, 'if one were clever at speaking, one could contrive a contest (*agon*) of conflicting arguments from everything',[32] and the evidence offered by Greek drama confirms the truth of this opinion. In the *Ajax* of Sophocles the captains of the Greeks debate whether or not to bury the body of Ajax, and it is this debate (verses 1047ff. and especially 1226ff.) which sustains our interest in the second part of the play. When, after a heated exchange of words, Menelaus leaves Teucer, the chorus anticipates what is to ensue by commenting that there will be a contest (*agon*) of great strife (verse 1163). In his *Electra* Sophocles depicts a Clytemnestra who attempts to justify the murder of Agamemnon, but receives an effective counter to her arguments from her daughter Electra (verses 516ff.), and this debate also features in Euripides' own *Electra* (verses 1011ff.). Jason and Medea catalogue the advantages they have bestowed on each other in the *Medea* (verses 459ff.) only for each to deny that these were advantages; that this is yet another contest (*hamilla*) of words is said explicitly by Jason (verse 546). Although one is convinced that this is a 'real' quarrel between man and woman, the formality of the debate is underlined by an exact correspondence in length between Medea's list of advantages (verses 465–519, 468 being thought spurious) and Jason's reply (verses 522–75). And it has been pointed out that in this scene from the *Medea* Euripides breaks his rule whereby the sympathetic character speaks second in the event of a quarrel. But there is an obvious reason for this exception, and this reason takes us back once more to the court of law. Usually the sympathetic character is cast in the role of the defendant, whereas in the *Medea* the sympathetic character, Medea of course, is prosecuting the case; in other words, the dramatist follows the procedure of the law court, in which the plaintiff usually spoke first. Links between drama and legal action, we may note in passing, go so far as to include a common use of the word *agon*, for in law we meet the classification *agones timetoi* and *atimetoi* to distinguish suits where the penalty was not fixed in advance by law and those where the penalty was already laid down.[33] In the *Trojan Women* Helen and Hecuba present

their case before a third party, Menelaus, who acts as arbitrator, and
private and public arbitrators were known to Athenian law; in fact all
male citizens had to undergo service as public arbitrators during the
official year which followed the year they became fifty-nine. Agamemnon
has to pronounce judgement when in the *Hecuba* Polymestor and the
Trojan queen in turn present their cases, the one for having murdered
Polydorus and the other for having extracted so frightful a revenge for
the murder (verses 1132ff. and 1187ff.). In the *Phoenissae* Jocasta listens
while Polyneices and Eteocles defend their respective actions in coming to
armed conflict (verses 452ff.).

The spectators who witnessed the exchanges which we have discussed
above or comparable scenes while sitting in the Theatre of Dionysus surely
qualified, to use Cleon's phrase, as 'spectators of sophists'. Verbal pyrotechnics and the sophists both suggest the art of rhetoric. The closeness of
rhetoric and poetry is made quite clear in Plato's *Gorgias*, when Callicles
and Socrates converse together, examining the purpose of tragic poetry
(502c–d). Here Socrates points out that poetry stripped of its song,
rhythm and metre consists just of 'words'. Pursuing the argument, the
philosopher maintains that, inasmuch as these words are directed to a
great throng of people, poetry is a kind of public speaking, and, even
more narrowly, rhetorical public speaking. Callicles has no hesitation in
replying in the affirmative when asked if poets in the theatre seem to him
to play the part of orators. Living proof that Callicles was right not to
hesitate is provided in the fourth century by the person of Theodectes,
for, in spite of an early death, Theodectes achieved fame as orator, expert
on rhetorical theory and tragedian. The versatility of Theodectes even by
our standards seems to have been considerable and for a Greek is quite
remarkable, but the emphasis in drama as much as in oratory on the spoken
word suggests strongly that such versatility was more apparent than real.
Aeschines was both orator and actor, albeit, in the opinion of his opponent
Demosthenes, a poor actor, while a tradition records that Demosthenes
himself was taught delivery by Polus the actor. In the assembly, in the
law-courts, and in the theatre the Athenian might enjoy performances
which were far from being dissimilar in style as well as in substance. The
spoken word was to be heard on every side.

NOTES

[1] Hart, op. cit. pp. 107–8.
[2] Hart, op. cit. p. 110.
[3] See W. B. Stanford, *The Sound of Greek* (Berkeley, 1967), pp. 36–38.
[4] B. L. Joseph, *Elizabethan Acting* (Oxford,[2] 1964), pp. 70–71. Joseph's statement is reassuring in view
    of the fact that Hart's estimate of time has recently been the subject of an attack mounted by David
    Klein, *Shakespeare Quarterly* 18 (1967), pp. 434–38.
[5] *Harvard Studies in Classical Philology* 60 (1951), pp. 23–59.

6 *Preface to Plato* (Oxford, 1963). Especially relevant is Havelock's third chapter 'Poetry as Preserved Communication'. A specific treatment of the impact of literacy on Greek culture is offered by Jack Goody and Ian Watt in J. Goody (ed.), *Literacy in Traditional Societies* (Cambridge, 1968), pp. 27–68. On the oral background of Shakespeare, see Bradbrook, *The Growth and Structure of Elizabethan Comedy*, especially pp. 21–26, and Terence Hawkes, *Shakespeare Survey* 24 (1971), pp. 47–54, and *Shakespeare's Talking Animals*, pp. 37ff., who comments, 'Shakespeare's plays must have been written for an audience of people who communicated primarily by talking and listening, whether they could read or not, and in situations of personal confrontation' (p. 49).

7 *Greek Studies* (Oxford, 1946), p. 22; cf. also *Journal of Hellenic Studies* 74 (1954), pp. 49ff.

8 Gladys D. Willcock, *Shakespeare Survey* 7 (1954), p. 20.

9 F. D. Harvey, *Revue des Études Grecques* 79 (1966), pp. 585–635.

10 J. A. Davison, *Phoenix* 16 (1962), p. 155 (cf. also p. 231).

11 The best introduction to the writings of Marshall McLuhan is *The Gutenberg Galaxy* (London, 1962). In its opening words the book is said to be in many respects complementary to A. B. Lord's *The Singer of Tales*, a work which discusses oral composition and the Homeric poems, and much that follows relates to antiquity and the Elizabethan period. One should, in addition, consult the writings of W. J. Ong, especially *The Presence of the Word* (New Haven and London, 1967), and *Rhetoric, Romance and Technology* (Ithaca and London, 1971). For the impact of printing see Elizabeth L. Eisenstein, *Past and Present* 45 (1969), pp. 19–89, and 52 (1971), pp. 140–44, and Theodore K. Rabb, *Past and Present* 52 (1971), pp. 135–40. Also relevant is Malcolm Bradbury, *The Social Context of Modern English Literature* (Oxford, 1971), especially pp. 171ff.

12 Cf. J. P. Lynch, *Aristotle's School, a Study of a Greek Educational Institution* (Berkeley, 1972), pp. 83ff.

13 See B. M. W. Knox, *Greek, Roman and Byzantine Studies* 9 (1968), pp. 421–35.

14 Compare the critical discussion of Euripides' *Hippolytus* by Knox, *Yale Classical Studies* 13 (1952), pp. 1–31, and Anne Barton on 'Shakespeare and the Limits of Language', *Shakespeare Survey* 24 (1971), pp. 19–30.

15 Peter Arnott, *Greek Scenic Conventions in the Fifth Century B.C.* (Oxford, 1962), pp. 134–38; see also Arnott's discussion of the suicide of Ajax, pp. 131–33.

16 G. F. Else, *The Origin and Early Form of Greek Tragedy* (Cambridge, Mass., 1965), pp. 51ff., my quotation being taken from page 69.

17 Aristotle's comment has now been re-examined by B. R. Rees, *Greece and Rome* 19 (1972), pp. 1–11.

18 See T. B. L. Webster, *The Tragedies of Euripides* (London, 1967), pp. 171–72, but compare an earlier remark on page 142.

19 *Moralia* 998 E. The scene is also referred to by Aristotle, *Poetics* 1454a 5–7.

20 *On Style* 195.

21 Frag. 442 Pearson. But see now W. S. Barrett in Richard Carden, *The Papyrus Fragments of Sophocles* (Berlin/New York, 1974), pp. 171ff. and especially pp. 184–85.

22 *Sophocles, Oedipus the King*, Minnesota Drama Editions no. 8, Minneapolis, 1972.

23 A. M. Dale, *Collected Papers* (Cambridge, 1969), p. 268; cf. M. D. Reeve, *Greek, Roman and Byzantine Studies* 13 (1972), pp. 263–64.

24 On the comic tone in Euripides' later plays, see Knox in *The Rarer Action, Essays in Honor of Francis Fergusson*, New Brunswick, 1971, pp. 68–96.

25 F. A. Paley in his edition of the plays of Euripides, vol. II, London, 1858, p. xxvii.

26 See R. Sri Pathmanathan, *Greece and Rome* 12 (1965), pp. 2–14, who argues convincingly that dramatic considerations account for off-stage death in Greek tragedy, and that Ajax and Evadne commit suicide on stage.

27 The appearance of the Furies is considered by P. G. Maxwell-Stuart, *Greece and Rome* 20 (1973), pp. 81–84.

28 Bernard Beckerman, *Shakespeare at the Globe 1599–1609* (New York, 1962), pp. 136–37.

29 On the chorus and its 'decline', see Dale, op. cit. pp. 210ff.

30 Haigh, op. cit. p. 226.

31 See on these lines W. K. G. Guthrie, *A History of Greek Philosophy III* (Cambridge, 1969), p. 43 n. 4.

32 These lines from the *Antiope* (frag. 189 Nauck²) introduce Jacqueline Duchemin's L'ΑΓΩΝ *dans la Tragédie grecque* (Paris,² 1968), a book which considers the *agon* as a dramatic device exhaustively, especially valuable being the third part of this study 'étude technique', pp. 136ff; see also *Dioniso* 43 (1969), pp. 247–75.

33 Full details of Athenian legal procedure will be found in A. R. W. Harrison, *The Law of Athens, Procedure* (Oxford, 1971). The 'agonistic' character of Greek society is everywhere apparent, not only in organized competitions, both dramatic and athletic, and the law, but also in war, on which see Jean-Pierre Vernant, *Mythe et Société en Grèce ancienne* (Paris, 1974), pp. 45ff.

Actors and Acting I

So far we have argued that a Greek play was performed in antiquity more rapidly than a play of equivalent length would be performed in the contemporary theatre. Time is consumed as a speech is delivered, but speed of delivery is determined by the rate at which an audience comprehends the spoken word, and Greek spectators are likely to have followed the sense, felt the impact, of words delivered by an actor at a greater speed than is customary today, for our culture is dominated by the printed word and we have sacrificed the habit of concentrated listening. But Greek drama, it will be remembered, contains two elements, actors and chorus. The *Agamemnon*, an abnormally long play by the standard set by the other surviving plays of Aeschylus, includes the longest choral ode known to us (verses 40–263), but a lack of evidence makes it impossible to assess variation in pace of performance when chorus sings (and dances) or actors recite. Guesswork is no substitute for knowledge, and there is little consistency in the estimates made by scholars who mention the time needed for the performance of particular Greek choral odes.[1] What we can do, however, is to reach some necessarily tentative conclusions about the style of acting practised in the fifth century B.C., and these conclusions will have wider implications for the understanding of Greek drama as well as a relevance to the problem of length of time consumed by performances in the Theatre of Dionysus. That there were in the fifth century recognizable standards by which acting skill might be assessed is made evident by two facts: first, in 449 B.C. a competiton for the protagonists (chief actors) at each City Dionysia was instituted, and a competition of this kind between actors implies some means by which acting ability may be judged, as also does the Elizabethan practice of acting for wagers;[2] secondly, actors could criticize fellow-performers, as those actors of the older school are said by Aristotle to have commented unfavourably on the antics of their successors—Mynniscus dubbed Callipides an ape because he 'went too far' (*Poetics* 146lb 33–35), and, irrespective of the precise grounds of his criticism, the very fact that Mynniscus could complain about a colleague's performance is not devoid of significance.

Time passes as action is portrayed on the stage, as actors act out their roles, and the art of acting today takes advantage not only of action but also of non-action, since the meaningful pause is frequently exploited in the contemporary theatre. In our own theatre the standard style of acting to be seen attempts to reproduce as closely as possible what we may call natural human behaviour. But are we to believe that the Greek actor of the fifth century B.C. aspired to an exact reproduction of life and action even to the extent of falling flat on the stage if this is what the situation demanded? It seems that Haigh would have us think so, for although on one page of his study of the Greek theatre he claims that 'the nature of the tragic actor's dress was sufficient in itself to make a realistic type of acting impossible', yet, on the same page and only a few lines on, he says of actors that 'they could even fall flat on the ground'.[3] While their view of the actor's costume does not prevent them from a belief that the portrayal of violent action was possible, Gould and Lewis strike a note of caution: 'If we remember the undoubted fact that facial expressions such as weeping, which were certainly not visible on stage, are frequently described in the plays, we must at least reckon with the possibility that the descriptions of striking and vigorous movement that we meet in the plays are not unequivocal evidence for the occurrence of these same movements in a naturalistic performance by the actor'.[4] Certainly passages may describe action of a surprisingly vigorous type, and anything like a style of realistic acting would compel us to add a generous allocation to the time which would in any case be spent in the simple delivery of the text, rather more time in fact than Hart is prepared to allow for the beginning of *Romeo and Juliet* (see our p. 20).

It will be best to commence a discussion of Greek acting with the obvious, that is, the example cited by Gould and Lewis. In the Greek theatre it was not the actor playing the role of a tearful character who conveyed to the audience an impression that he was crying; it was another character on the stage or the chorus, who, by remarking that so-and-so was in tears, informed the spectators of that fact. The size of the theatre and the consequent distance from acting area to the furthermost seats, and the semi-circular shape of the theatre with its relatively poor sight-lines restricted the power of the audience to see with precision; but even if we credited each member of the audience with the eyes of a Lynceus, he would not be able to see a Greek actor on the stage weeping, for, and here I repeat what has often been observed, change of facial expression is denied the actor who wears a mask. When in the *Antigone* Sophocles' Ismene enters the stage in tears, the chorus must tell us that the woman is crying (verse 527). When the chorus says, 'Here's Ismene before the gates' (verse 526), we have a stage-direction, but the following line is no stage direction inserted for the benefit of a producer. A Greek producer, reading verse 526 of his script, could say to the actor playing the part of Ismene, 'As the chorus delivers this line, you come on stage', but, proceeding to the next verse, he could not say, 'As the chorus delivers this line, cry', for this instruction would be to demand an impossibility from a masked actor. This scene from the *Antigone* may be brief, but to suggest that the mask worn by Ismene during it might have been appropriately tearful is a desperate effort to impose our own standards of realism on the Greeks,[5] and a suggestion, furthermore, which conveniently ignores other instances and longer scenes in the extant plays of Sophocles when characters are said to shed tears; later in the *Antigone*, for example, the whole chorus cannot restrain from a flood of tears (verse 803) and the chorus, of course, remains in full view of the spectators throughout the action of the play after the opening scene. A sorrowful Ismene poses a problem which might not be so acute if the emotion she was experiencing was one of joy. When Creon early in the *Oedipus Tyrannus* returns with good news from Delphi, his approach is noted by the priest (verses 78–79). It becomes apparent from the words of Oedipus that Creon's eyes are shining, a fair enough indication of a satisfactory consultation at the oracle (verse 81). And, while Creon's eyes cannot in fact shine, his success is clearly implied because he wears a wreath of laurel (verses 82–83). This piece of stage property is not elaborate but it makes its point most effectively, adding a touch of verisimilitude which, in an unsophisticated form, no Greek dramatist scorned. Thus in the *Ajax* the chorus refers to the arrival of an enemy, and, when Teucer asks who this is, he is told that it is Menelaus. Before the Greek king addresses his first words to the audience, Teucer states that he sees him 'for, being nearby, he is not difficult to recognize' (verses 1042–46), and such an exchange between chorus and actor not only provides time for Menelaus to come upon the stage, but also creates the impression that it really is Menelaus, who 'in the distance' cannot be identified but is recognized once he joins Teucer at or near the centre of the stage.

We must never forget that the Greek actor sported a mask and thus was denied the opportunity to exploit any range of facial expressions. But can this line of argument be further developed? It may be if Alfred Harbage's case for formal, rather than natural, acting in the Elizabethan theatre is next considered.[6] It need hardly be said that masks were not worn by the Elizabethans, but Harbage isolates another type of passage where, he claims, particular effects were created not by acting on the part of the performer but by description of the performer, citing from Sprague Brutus' description in *Julius Caesar* (1.2) of 'the angry spot' glowing on Caesar's brow, Calpurnia's pale cheek and Cicero's 'ferret' and 'fiery' eyes.[7] Seemingly pertinent questions and what seems to be an equally pertinent conclusion follow: 'Did an angry spot actually glow on Caesar's brow? Did Calpurnia's cheek turn pale, Caesar's (a mistake presumably for 'Cicero's') eyes fiery? Did Hamlet's hair actually stand 'on end? Unless we think so, we must qualify the declarations of the actor speaking, until they lose all significance as indications of what his fellow actors are doing.'

Not content with the evidence offered by the Elizabethan theatre, Harbage quotes Sophocles' *Philoctetes* when Neoptolemus describes Philoctetes sinking into sleep (verses 821-26):

> In a little while, I think,
> sleep will come on this man. His head is nodding.
> The sweat is soaking all his body over,
> and a black flux of blood and matter has broken
> out of his foot. Let us leave him quiet, friends,
> until he falls asleep.[8]

It is scarcely credible that the Greek cast in the role of the stricken Philoctetes could have produced such effects as trickling sweat and oozing blood, and so what Harbage says of the Elizabethan theatre appears at first thought to be also applicable to its ancient counterpart: 'The descriptive element in the Elizabethan dramatic line, far from being evidence of natural acting, is the exact reverse. It indicates that the speaker, not the speaker's fellow-actors, was charged with the task of implanting an image in the minds of the auditors.' We may picture the audience's attention concentrated on the speaker of the moment to the exclusion of his silent colleague, on Neoptolemus, in this example, and not on Philoctetes, since it is what the former says, and not what the latter does, which creates an image in the mind. Granted that an actor is an ordinary person, he may not bleed at will. Neoptolemus then is not detailing the actions of an actor playing the part of Philoctetes, but the imagined reactions of the true Philoctetes, marooned on a deserted island and stricken down with a horrid wound.

At this point it is convenient to recall that our evidence suggests that the Greek theatre was characterized by nothing, or very little, in the way of scenery. Actual scenery is replaced by verbal description, most obviously in a drama whose locale is not the usual palace or temple set, when the stage-building itself offers an adequate substitute for the scenery of the modern theatre. The illusion that the stage-building is a palace or temple or even some other kind of structure may be reinforced by making a character speak off-stage, that is, from inside the stage-building, but this is not essential. The two *Oedipus* plays by Sophocles provide us with a contrast, one exhibiting a standard and the other a less orthodox setting. In the *Oedipus Tyrannus* we learn from Oedipus' opening words (verses 1-8), supplemented by remarks passed by the Priest (cf. verses 15-16, 19-21 and 32), that the suppliants are seated before the royal palace in the city of Thebes, but there is no call for additional details. The *Oedipus Coloneus* is not localized before a palace or temple, and we must, therefore, have the setting described at greater length. At the same time such information is much more limited in scope than is verbal description in the Elizabethan theatre, but in the latter case the setting tends to be more 'exotic', being outside the range of knowledge and experience of the audience, while the setting changes from scene to scene and each setting will demand more or less in the way of description. Since Oedipus is blind, there is nothing incongruous in a more detailed account of the setting of the *Oedipus Coloneus*: we are near a city (cf. verses 14–15), actually Athens (verse 24), in a grove (verses 16–18) of the Eumenides (verses 39–40 and 42) at Colonus (verses 58–61). There is more than basic information here, since the grove is described as being full of laurel, olive and vine and haunted by nightingales (verses 16–18), and this description is later to be vastly elaborated by the chorus in the Colonus ode (verses 668ff.). We appear to see here the application of a principle of economy. A modern play will be presented on the stage with whatever scenery is appropriate, and there is also the theatre programme. And so there is no need for verbal description of the setting. The front of the stage-building supplies the *Oedipus Tyrannus* with all the scenery the play requires, and the information quickly conveyed early in the play adds up to the type of information a modern theatre-goer finds in his programme. In the other *Oedipus* play we have neither scenery nor a usual kind of setting, and the result is that altogether more information is conveyed by what is said, and the chorus perhaps is the best agent to convey such information.

We would be wrong to exaggerate the element of verbal description characteristic of Greek drama even when the play is not set before palace or temple. The traditional material offered by mythological plots and personal knowledge eliminate the necessity for excessive elaboration. In one play which has survived, of course, there is a change of location within the drama itself. Aeschylus' *Eumenides* opens at Apollo's temple at Delphi, but the audience is transported after verse 234 to Athens and the Areopagus.[9] The transition is abrupt, for all we have is a brief speech of nine lines from Orestes, in which he announces his arrival in obedience to Apollo's commands at Athene's 'house and statue' (verses 235–43), followed by lines from the chorus which clearly denote pursuit (verses 244ff.). It is the statue of Athene before which Orestes sits (cf. verses 409, 439–41 and 446) that offers the audience a new focus for its attention, and the journey from Delphi to Athens must be imagined on the basis of a relatively few words, coupled with some movement from one to another part of the performing area.

We spoke above of a principle of economy—setting will either be depicted by scenery or described in words, but have also seen that verbal description is not all that common in Greek drama. Did a comparable principle of economy apply to acting as well? Are we to believe that action was either carried out or described as if it were being carried out, and that these are mutually exclusive techniques? If this is indeed true, then, the evidence provided by the use of masks and Harbage's example from the *Philoctetes* suggest that Greek acting was far removed from being naturalistic. Yet Harbage's argument when applied to Greek drama cannot be sustained, and the reason I say this is a simple one: there are very few passages in Greek tragedy when a character is described as doing something, performing an action, which is physically impossible for an actor. In the *Trachiniae* of Sophocles Heracles' agony when he puts on the poisoned robe is reported by Hyllus (verses 765ff.), and when he is carried onto the stage and then wakes up (verses 964ff.), Heracles, although in extreme pain, is coherent (verses 983ff.) and does nothing beyond the capabilities of a very average actor. The ravings of Ajax occur off-stage, being related before the audience by Tecmessa (verses 296ff.), and the hero has recovered his senses in Sophocles' play by the time he comes on-stage (verses 348ff.); it is what he did when off-stage, and not his actions on the stage, which argues for insanity, and, even when on the point of suicide (verses 815ff.), he remains rational and his actions would tax no actor's powers, however moderate the actor's talents. In the *Philoctetes* Philoctetes registers a considerable variety of emotions—joy when he learns that the strangers are Greek and when he thinks he is to be returned to Greece by Neoptolemus (verses 234ff. and 530ff.); anguish at the onset of pain (verses 732ff.); a mixture of fury and pathos when he thinks himself to be betrayed (verses 927ff.); unadulterated fury when Odysseus appears and threatens to carry him off (verses 1004ff.); and despair (verses 1081ff.). Yet to depict emotion is the actor's stock-in-trade. Perhaps a variation in tone and strength of delivery might have conveyed all that was necessary, though this I am inclined to doubt; the fact that an actor might have to undertake several contrasting roles, that of someone young and someone old, that of a man and that of a woman, in the course of the same play rather suggests a measure of restriction on a natural use of the voice. The blood inclined to ooze from the wound of Philoctetes is mentioned by Odysseus early in the drama (verse 7) and later elicits a comment from the chorus (verses 696ff.); his foot actually drips blood on the stage only at two points in the play, the passage cited by Harbage, that is, verses 821–26, and slightly earlier when Philoctetes himself refers to the flow (verses 783–84). The very fact that it is Philoctetes who is speaking in the earlier passage tends to destroy the force of Harbage's argument and the resultant conclusion. Philoctetes, of course, is stricken but alive. The body of the dead Ajax is conveniently and quickly covered up by

Tecmessa (verses 915–19); it may still bleed (cf. verses 1411–13), but this display of gore is not inflicted on the audience.

When the mangled body of Euripides' Hippolytus is returned to the stage, the young prince is in agony but not extravagantly so (*Hippolytus*, 1347ff.), and the arrival of Artemis brings relief from pain (verses 1392ff.). Euripides offers a parallel to Calpurnia's paleness of cheek when Antigone in the *Phoenissae* speaks of the blush upon her face (verses 1487–88) and to Hamlet's hair standing on end when in the *Helen* Helen speaks of her hair also standing erect, although the emotion she experiences is joy and not fear (verses 632–33). The chorus in Aeschylus' *Seven against Thebes* speaks of its hair standing on end (verse 564) and here the emotion is one of terror (cf. also *Choephori*, 32); in Sophocles we have only a report of the same reaction to portentious happenings (*Oedipus Coloneus*, 1624–25). What about parallels to Cicero's fiery eyes? We have already noted that Creon's eyes are bright in the *Oedipus Tyrannus* (verse 81) when he returns to Thebes, having consulted the god Apollo, and so too are those of Ismene as she arrives in the *Oedipus Coloneus* (verses 319–20). The eyes of the children of Heracles in the *Hercules Furens* flash fiercely like those of their father (verses 130–32). Blood-shot eyes are referred to in the *Agamemnon* (verse 1428) and in the *Iphigenia in Aulis* (verse 381). But for the best parallel we should turn to Euripides' *Orestes*. The part of Orestes in this play is really the only role in the dramatist's surviving works to present its exponent with difficulties, and these are difficulties again associated with facial features. When first aroused from sleep Orestes is quiet and remembers nothing (verses 211ff.); there seems to have been foam about his mouth and eyes (verses 219–20), and his hair is matted and his face filthy (verses 223–26). After he has struggled to his feet with the help of Electra, he changes (verses 253ff.); his eyes grow wild and the Furies appear to be upon him. His deadly appearance, unkempt hair and the terrible look in his eyes are all the subject of comment on the part of the newly arrived Menelaus; 'Gods in heaven, is this some corpse I see?' (verse 385); 'And that wild, matted hair—how horrible you look!' (verse 387); 'That awful stare—and those dry, cold eyes . . .' (verses 389).[10]

To prove his case Harbage naturally chose a convincing example. It would seem, however, that, if we exclude from the list we have just been compiling examples which fall into the particular category of facial expression or features (and I use the adjective 'particular' bearing in mind the fact that masks were worn by Greek actors), Harbage, perhaps unwittingly, chose the very best, even the only, example when he singled out Philoctetes' wound. It is tempting, therefore, to reverse his argument and to conclude that the rarity of such examples strongly suggest that

Greek acting was naturalistic rather than formal. When allowance is made for the immense size of the ancient theatre, the use of masks seems less a restriction and more a convention derived from tradition which was retained because it was of little or no consequence, since free range of facial expression would add nothing to the effectiveness of an actor performing in so vast a theatre, an opinion, however, which we shall see at the end of this chapter, does not do full justice to the use of masks by the Greek dramatists. Certain knowledge as to how the Greek actor comported himself on the stage can be derived only from a contemporary or a near-contemporary, that is, a fifth or fourth-century, description of an actual theatrical performance and this, I need hardly say, we do not possess.[11]

But we do know something, although admittedly little, about the performance of rhapsodes at this period of time, and, whether or not a connection is acknowledged between dramatic recitations from the Homeric poems and the origins of drama, it is scarcely likely that actors performed with less naturalism than that associated with rhapsodes reciting the verses of Homer. Homer, according to Socrates in the *Republic* (392e ff.), opens the *Iliad* by speaking in his own person, but then proceeds as if he were Chryses himself and tries to create the impression that the person speaking is not the poet but the old priest. Certainly the idea of attempting to reproduce the likeness of another's voice is as old as Homer, since in *Odyssey* iv. 274ff. Helen is said to have circled the Wooden Horse when it stood outside Troy with its deadly cargo of Greek warriors and to have called out the names of the warriors, likening her voice to those of their wives (cf. also the Homeric *Hymn to Apollo*, 162–63). When a speech is delivered in the Homeric poems, it is readily agreed among Socrates and his fellows, the poet does his utmost to reproduce the authentic tone of the supposed speaker; in other words, Homer and the other poets fashion their narrative 'through imitation'. If the poet's own words which occur between the speeches are eliminated, you are left with the equivalent of a tragedy, which, together with comedy, operates entirely through imitation. At the end of the *Poetics* (146lb 26ff.) Aristotle evaluates the respective merits of epic and tragedy, concluding that tragedy is the superior. The argument that epic is directed at a cultivated audience which has no need of gestures and is, therefore, to be preferred is rejected, since this is a criticism of the art of the performer and not that of the dramatist. Furthermore, the recitation of epic may be ruined by an extravagant performance, not all movement is disreputable, and tragedy may produce its effect when divorced from movement, as it is when read and not seen in performance in a theatre. Whatever is felt about the claims of epic and tragedy as art-forms which compete for our approval, and whatever is felt about Aristotle's evaluation of their respective merits, the very fact that the philosopher saw fit to close his defence of dramatic poetry with such a comparison and the whole tone of his argument at this point stress how narrow a gap separates the two genres of poetry represented by Greek epic and Greek tragedy.

If Plato's ideal state should witness the arrival of a man able in his cleverness to assume any character and to imitate everything, and that man wishes to make a public display of his talents, he may be admired but he is also to be sent on his way once he has had his head anointed with oil and crowned with a fillet of wool (*Republic* 398a). Does Socrates have in mind a special category of person when he speaks so ironically of paying a kind of divine honour to one who is at the same time to be expelled from the philosopher's state? The description of the rhapsode in action which is encountered in Plato's dialogue the *Ion* certainly suggests that Socrates is thinking of the professional reciter of the Homeric poems. Ion himself leaves us in no doubt as to the rhapsode's personal reactions as he recites, dressed in an embroidered robe, decked with wreaths of gold, and facing a throng of more than 20,000, and as to the effect that his recitation has on the audience: Whenever I deliver a pathetic passage, Ion claims, my eyes brim with tears; whenever I deliver a passage terrifying or terrible, my hair stands on end and my heart bounds (535c). The spectators weep, gaze fiercely and are astounded as they respond to the performance (535e). The rhapsode must pay attention to his audience, evoking in the onlookers the appropriate emotion, for much is at stake— the rhapsode's livelihood! And the audience responds as Homer tells us Odysseus responded with tears (and the hero's response is reinforced by an elaborate simile) as he listened to Demodocus sing of the Wooden Horse (*Odyssey* viii. 521ff.). It is no occasion for surprise that the audience was so gripped with emotion, for Ion was just as much the victim of his own emotions. In fact, like Euripides and Agathon (see our pp. 8–10), though he was a performer and not the author, Ion was a living illustration of Aristotle's belief that 'given the same natural endowment, people who actually feel passion are the most convincing; that is, the person who most realistically expresses distress is the person in distress and the same is true of a person in a temper' (*Poetics* 1455a 30–32).

In his reply to Ion, Socrates couples together the rhapsode and the actor, and indeed Ion's statement finds parallels in the few comments upon actors and the effects of their performances to have reached us from antiquity.[12] Thus we read in Xenophon, a source contemporary with Plato, that Callippides, an actor we have already seen dubbed the monkey, took excessive pride in his ability to reduce his audience to tears (*Sym.* iii. 11), a comment which reveals that the actor Callippides and the rhapsode

Ion shared the same purpose, to set their audience down weeping. Another actor Theodorus, when playing the part of Merope 'with extremely deep emotion' in Euripides' *Cresphontes*, caused as savage a tyrant as Alexander of Pherae to burst into tears and to bound from the theatre, ashamed that he was able to feel pity for the sufferings depicted by actors but not those of his own people.[13] A story recorded about the actor Polus is suggestive, for it clearly implies that an actor could 'live' his part: Polus, who had lost a beloved son, used the real remains of the child to carry in the urn when appearing in the role of Sophocles' Electra, and had no need to simulate the grief which Electra experienced when led to believe that her brother had perished (A. Gell. vi. 5). The fact that Polus substituted the ashes of his own son for any form of stage property brings us to a crucial issue. Polus' own experience of life and the imagined experience of the character he portrayed on the stage happened to coincide, but it cannot be expected that such an occurrence will often arise. However wide his experience of life, every actor faces one form of restriction: he can only be as good a performer as his part allows, and the scope allowed by a role depends not only upon the dramatic ability of the playwright but also upon the type and degree of characterization permitted within each theatrical tradition. Acting among the Greeks was an exclusively male profession and the Greek actor might well find himself playing several parts in the same play, as might also the Elizabethan actor, who again had to undertake the role of women as well as male characters. Thus in the *Agamemnon* two actors divide between them the parts other than that of Clytemnestra, that is, the Watchman, Herald, Agamemnon, Cassandra and Aegisthus.[14] In Sophocles' *Antigone* two actors taken on between them the parts other than that of Creon and possibly Eurydice, namely the parts of Antigone, Ismene, the Guard, Haemon, Teiresias and the two Messengers, while in the *Trojan Women* of Euripides two actors share the parts of Poseidon, Athene, Talthybius, Cassandra, Andromache, Menelaus and Helen, a total of seven roles as in the case of the *Antigone*. Clearly actors might well be called upon to play a number of 'characters' in the same drama, and these characters might well represent very different types with some, for example, male and others female roles, some young and others old parts. But there is yet a further complication: perhaps in the *Oedipus Coloneus* and again in the *Phoenissae* a part might be divided during the course of the play between two different actors.

Greek plays, as we have been seeing, were brief, and the fact that a play is named after a particular character appearing in the play is no guarantee that such a character dominates the drama throughout by his or her physical presence on the stage. After all, it is late in the

Agamemnon before the king appears on the stage, and even then he does not remain there for long before being hurried off to his death; Antigone disappears from the stage and from our eyes, if not from our thoughts, when Sophocles' tragedy of the same name is merely two-thirds complete; Andromache seems to leave the stage in Euripides' *Andromache* after verse 765, or, if she is on stage, she has nothing to do or to say. If a play is brief, the parts allotted the actors are correspondingly brief, especially in the Greek theatre with its choral odes, and this must affect the scope permitted characterization. It is true that in the *Oresteia* trilogy Clytemnestra is featured in all three plays which make up the trilogy. Irrespective of the question whether or not the same actor played the role of Clytemnestra in all three plays, this does seem altogether more of a part and one is inclined to imagine that it offered some scope for character development and not only because the part is a more substantial one—in the first play Clytemnestra murders her husband, in the second she begs her son Orestes for her own life but fails to move him, and in the *Eumenides* she appears as a ghost intent on revenge. This change in fortune and these very different circumstances suggest that some modification in the attitude of Clytemnestra is likely, but the queen in fact remains very much the same throughout the trilogy though her position is so different, and we are left to conclude that the conventions which typify Greek drama include what is to some extent at least a conventional presentation of characters. We tend to associate stock situations and stock characters with the later New Comedy, but this ought not to blind us to the fact that the myths which provide the tragedians with their material are limited in number and in range of subject-matter (cf. *Poetics* 1453a 17ff.), and that, secondly, fifth-century drama also deals in some 'stock' characters, most obviously where the inevitable messenger, who may or may not be individualized and often is not, is concerned and the choruses, the status of whose constituent members is not all that varied.[15]

One of the most frequently encountered character-types in Greek tragedy is the tyrant. It has been pointed out by Dodds how Pentheus in the *Bacchae* of Euripides is presented as 'a typical tragedy-tyrant', since he is devoid of self-control, is willing to believe the worst on hearsay evidence or none, is brutal towards the helpless, and stupidly relies on physical force to settle spiritual problems. These general characteristics are supplemented by a couple of particular traits, a foolish racial pride and what is termed the sexual curiosity of a Peeping Tom.[16] To what extent is Dodds justified in referring to a typical tragedy-tyrant figure? An effective test is supplied by consideration of two other 'tyrants', Oedipus in *Oedipus Tyrannus* and Creon in the *Antigone*, and I single out these two examples because we are apt to heap abuse on the head of Creon in the latter play but to sympathize with the dilemma of Oedipus in the former, whereas both in fact conform to the tyrant-type as identified in the *Bacchae*. On the basis of the criteria listed above Oedipus certainly qualifies as an example of the conventional tyrant. His lack of self-control is abundantly illustrated in his clash with the prophet Teiresias (see especially verses 334ff.); his own description (verses 800ff.) of the meeting with Laius at the cross-roads, an encounter which ended with the wholesale slaughter of the other side (verse 813), hardly argues for a man noted for his restraint. Tyrants suffer from 'the Sword of Damocles' complex, suspecting conspiracy against their regime, however fragile the actual evidence of a plot, and Oedipus is no stranger to any such phobia (cf. verses 137–41). Oedipus is very ready to believe the worst, suspecting Teiresias of being involved in a plot with Creon as his accomplice (verses 346–49, 378, 385ff. and 399–400); when Creon reappears, having heard of the groundless accusation, the chorus comments that the charge might have been the result of rage rather than judgement (verses 523–24), and this suggestion, of course, is very close to the truth. When Oedipus and Creon come face to face, the tyrant savagely denounces his brother-in-law as if the existence of a conspiracy were a matter of established fact. The evidence, that it was at Creon's suggestion that Teiresias was consulted (verses 555–56), is flimsy and easily dismissed by Creon (verses 577ff.), but this merely causes Oedipus to become more incensed and exile is no longer sufficient punishment and Creon must be put to death (verses 622–23). It will also be remembered that the departure of Oedipus from Corinth was occasioned by suspicions equally fragile, an accusation of illegitimacy made by a man deep in his cups (verses 779–80), and indignant reaction on the part of Oedipus' supposed parents was insufficient to prevent such an insult from persistently bothering the hero. Indeed, if Oedipus possesses a particular trait, it is his obsessive preoccupation with his own birth and the possibility of it being anything less than respectable (cf. verses 437, 1062ff. and 1076ff.). Oedipus exhibits brutality towards the helpless when he cross-examines the old herdsman, who is reluctant to reveal the truth which will destroy the king of Thebes (see especially verses 1152–66), and so conforms to another of Dodds' criteria for the typical tragedy-tyrant.

Creon's first words in the *Antigone* are impressive (verses 163ff.), but he is soon to show his true colours when the first burial of Polyneices is reported by the Guard and the chorus suggests the presence of the hand of god (verses 280ff.). Again conspiracy is suspected (verses 289ff.) and the corrupting blight of bribery denounced (cf. already verses 221–22). Creon's self-control breaks down rapidly when he is opposed by a mere woman and one, moreover, who is a member of his own family and revels in her 'crime' (verses 441ff.), and later when the opposition comes from Haemon, his actual son (verses 726ff.); no greater command over his personal emotions is allowed Creon when he clashes angrily with the prophet Teiresias (verses 1033ff.). The evidence on the basis of which Creon assumes the complicity of Ismene in the burial of the brother (verses 489ff. and 531ff.), this woman's evident distress, is weak to the point of being virtually non-existent. A callous brutality directed against those in no position to defend themselves is illustrated by the threats with which Creon dismisses the unfortunate Guard (verses 305ff.), his response when Ismene remarks that Antigone and Haemon are betrothed; 'there are other fields to plough' (verse 569), his proposal that Antigone should be put to death on the spot in the sight of Haemon (verses 760–61), and his substitution of a slow death for the original punishment of death by stoning (verses 773–80; cf. verse 36). Both Creon and Oedipus, of course, reappear in the *Oedipus Coloneus*, but in this last play by Sophocles only Creon is now tyrant and the presentation of this character is also conditioned by the desire to draw as strong a contrast as possible with another ruler, Theseus, the national hero of Athens, who must be as good as Creon is hypocritical and wicked. It is Theseus in this drama and again in the *Supplices* of Euripides, Theseus' son Demophon in the *Heraclidae* and the king of Argos in Aeschylus' *Supplices* (see especially verses 911ff.) who alone do not conform to a type whose characteristics are sketched for us in the fifth century by the historian Herodotus (iii. 80), and it is national pride which explains the existence of three such exceptions to what is otherwise very much a fixed rule.

It is the existence in Greek drama of distinct types, of which the tyrant is one example, which enables us to understand Aristotle's requirement in the *Poetics* that 'the characters represented should be suitable' (1454a 22–24). Later we shall find ourselves considering the way in which the social values of fifth-century Athens are reflected in the plays of the Greek tragedians: for the Athenian, women were different from men and different in a manner which we would not recognize today; the two sexes represented different types and each type had its own particular qualities and virtues, so that what was expected of a woman was not the same as what was expected of a man. It was men, for example, and not women, who were required to be brave and clever, and the dramatist presented on the stage persons who conformed to their own characteristic type, age and social status being as much essential elements to the type as sex. In his discussion of Aristotle John Jones has clearly shown that the Greek dramatist was concerned not with the tragic hero or the individual in his own right but with 'the realised type'.[17] Jones develops his argument further, and in doing this brings us back to the point at which this chapter commenced, the use of masks in ancient drama. The mask has certainly obvious advantages: it enables an actor, for instance, to play more than a single role in a play. But this and other practical merits are of secondary importance; infinitely more significant is the fact that in indicating sex, age, race and social status the mask was able to convey just as much as the dramatist wished to convey in depicting the persons in his play. The mask could do all the dramatist wanted to be done, a positive statement of the coincidence between mask and concept of character which is to be preferred to the negative formulation that characters are as conventional as the masks featured in Greek drama. Jones makes the point more elegantly and more searchingly: 'Prosōpon, the Greek word for mask, also means face, aspect, person and stage-figure (persona); we should allow mask and face to draw semantically close together, and then we should enrich the face far beyond our own conception, until it is able to embrace (as it did for Greeks from the time of Homer) the look of a man together with the truth about him.'[18]

The discussion of the significance of the actor's mask by Jones led T. B. L. Webster to attempt to answer two other questions—'Did the poet regard the mask as a means of conveying his conception of the character to the actor, and did the actor accept this transference?'[19] The evidence offered by a statement of Quintilian when this critic says that 'skilled speakers borrow their emotions from the masks', and a reference by Fronto to the effect that the actor Aesopus 'conformed his gestures and voice to the face of the mask' confirms that the actor 'seems to have respected the mask as conveying to him the poet's interpretation of the character', and thus the second question is answered. The information to be gleaned from artistic representations of the poet with a mask or masks not only supplies a similarly affirmative answer to the first question, but also reveals that the poet uses the mask 'to fix his own conception of the character in the words that he gives to the character'. Here Webster refers initially to a grave-relief of a comic poet, possibly Aristophanes himself, which depicts a seated poet with papyrus in one hand and a slave mask in the other. As the poet writes, it seems, he contemplates the mask, and it is the mask which provides inspiration. In this case, as in the case of other evidence collected and cited by Webster, we have the final process in the composition of a play depicted by the artist: having constructed the plot, the dramatist, be it Sophocles or Menander, needs only to write the verses; the plot supplies the characters, and the characters determine which masks are to be selected from the poet's box of masks; with these masks before him, the poet completes his work of composition by writing the speeches. Webster rejects the view that special masks were produced for each and every part. There was a stock of standard masks, though such a stock was not fixed for all times and changes might be made as when the *onkos*, described by Webster as 'the triangular tower of hair above the forehead', was introduced. But there was a stock of masks, and, as the mask moulded the conception of character, so too stock rather than individual characters were conceived. In other words, the detailed evidence examined by Webster strengthens the case put by Jones that mask and stage-person are inextricably bound together with one supplementing and expanding the other. Mask and stage-person are one and the same, and mask and stage-person, moreover, represent stock types.

We began our discussion with the actor's mask and now we finish with this same convention. We certainly have not reached anything like a conclusion to our investigation of actors and acting in Greek drama. Foundations, however, have been laid, and we must proceed to build on those foundations in the hope that we shall later be able to form an altogether clearer picture of the type of acting style practised among the Greeks. Our expectation should be modest and our final conclusions tentative. If we avoid the dangers of an excessive ambition, we shall stand a better chance of deepening our understanding of the Greeks and their dramatic tradition, for, as what has been discussed already shows us, an investigation of acting techniques also demands that we consider the scope for characterization allowed by the dramatic tradition of the Greeks.

NOTES

1 What I really object to are unsubstantiated statements, such as that made by E. B. Pettet in *Classical Drama and its Influence*, edited by M. J. Anderson (London, 1965), p. 232, who refers to the second choral ode in the *Antigone* as 'a matter of some forty-four lines of approximately ten minutes in stage time'.
2 See Joseph, op. cit. pp. 93–95.
3 Haigh, op. cit. p. 276.
4 Gould and Lewis, op. cit. p. 176.
5 Gould and Lewis, op. cit. p. 172 n. 1.
6 A. Harbage, *Theatre for Shakespeare* (Toronto, 1955), pp. 92ff.
7 Harbage, ibid. pp. 106–8.
8 I quote the translation by David Grene in *The Complete Greek Tragedies, Sophocles II* (Chicago, 1957), p. 227.
9 For the staging at Athens of the plays of Aeschylus, now see N. G. L. Hammond, *Greek, Roman and Byzantine Studies* 13 (1972), pp. 387–450.
10 The translation quoted is that by William Arrowsmith in the fourth Euripides volume of the Chicago *The Complete Greek Tragedies* series (1958), p. 133.
11 The scanty evidence offered by fifth-century vase painting is detailed by Gerhard Neumann, *Gesten und Gebärden in der griechischen Kunst* (Berlin, 1965). See also A. D. Trendall and T. B. L. Webster, *Illustrations of Greek Drama* (London, 1971).
12 The relevant evidence has been collected in the appendix 'Prosopographia Histrionum Graecorum' of J. B. O'Connor, *Chapters in the History of Actors and Acting in Ancient Greece* (Chicago, 1908), pp. 68ff., which has since been brought up-to-date by Iride Parenti, *Dioniso* 35 (1961), pp. 5–29.
13 Aelian *V.H.* xiv. 40; cf. also Plutarch, *Mor.* 334 A.
14 For the distribution of parts between the actors in particular plays, see Gould and Lewis, op. cit. pp. 138ff.
15 See chapter XII 'Die Rollencharakteristik', pp. 79–85, of Anna Spitzbarth, *Untersuchungen zur Spieltechnik der griechischen Tragödie* (Zürich, 1946).
16 E. R. Dodds makes the point in his edition of the *Bacchae* (Oxford, 1944), p. xl.
17 *On Aristotle and Greek Tragedy* (London, 1962), pp. 38ff.
18 Jones, ibid. p. 44.
19 In *Classical Drama and its Influence* (see note 1 above), pp. 5–13. Webster's literary references are to Quin. xi. 3. 73 and Fronto, *de Eloqu.* i.17.

Actors and Acting II

THE myths dramatized by the tragedians already existed and the main lines of their plots were laid down. Characters must do certain things, even in defiance of what might seem their natural disposition: thus, in the *Antigone* of Sophocles, Creon must change his mind, burying Polyneices and releasing Antigone (see below), however abrupt that change of mind appears to be. For Aristotle it is action which is important and scholars commenting on the philosopher have been quick to point out the extent to which we are still the heirs of the nineteenth century when the novel, and the novel, moreover, of a monumental length, was the dominant literary form. We are still inclined to ask questions of the type represented by the notorious 'How many children had Lady Macbeth?', and are disappointed that an answer is impossible, forgetting that the priorities of the Greek tragedian are carefully enunciated by Aristotle and that 'the arrangement of the incidents' (*ta pragmata kai ho muthos*) is of prime consideration.[1] The characters in a play certainly must be credible, but in Greek drama the plot comes first and supplies the characters.

A strong warning has been voiced by A. M. Dale, who underlines the point that 'this notion of the "creation of character" is so familiar to us that we are liable to assume that all dramatists at all periods are concerned with it in the same sort of way, and even that it is an end in itself'. Much of the evidence, or so-called evidence, on the basis of which scholars have built up a picture, accompanied by subtle analysis, of character X is in no sense real evidence, but simply the critic's unwillingness to acknowledge that Greek drama has a certain, and a limited, number of standard ways or conventions by means of which characters express their feelings and opinions while on stage. Dale found it easy to provide illustrations of the distortion which is inevitable when what is said by a character is thought to reflect a conscious attempt at characterization by the playwright, and it is no more difficult to extend her list of such illustrations.[2] Dale's approach to the problem of characterization may be relatively new for the classics specialist, but this is not true of his counterpart in English studies. The views of the Shakespearean scholar Stoll, expressed in the thirties, are comparable.[3] For Stoll the core of drama is situation (pp. 1ff.), and 'when, as with the ancients and the Elizabethans, an old story was used anew, then, obviously, the plot came foremost in time and the characters were invented to fit it'. Having quoted Aristotle on the primacy of plot, Stoll maintains that the best situation is that which offers the most striking contrast or conflict, 'the probability or psychological reasonableness of it being a secondary consideration. Indeed, in the greatest tragedies . . . the situation has been fundamentally improbable, unreasonable.' Life is too deficient and too slow so as to allow the sharpest contrast or conflict, and 'to genius the improbability is only a challenge'. As Aristotle phrases it, 'if the poem contains an impossibility, that is a fault; but it is all right if the poem thereby achieves what it aims at, that is, if in this way the surprise produced either by that particular passage or by another is more striking' (*Poetics* 1460b 23–26).

Othello, for Stoll, is devoid of jealousy until the temptation, and then, although the accusation is unsupported by evidence or even likely, the Moor succumbs to jealousy; this is impossible psychology but may be understood as the result of a convention, the convention that one believes 'at the critical moment the detrimental thing that is cunningly told' (p. 6). Stoll identifies parallels from other theatrical traditions and these include Euripides' *Hippolytus* (see also p. 57); if Phaedra's suicide adds weight to her condemnation of her stepson, this is just because the accusation is 'cunningly told'. With Othello our difficulty is occasioned by the transition, from Othello not showing any signs of jealousy and a jealous disposition to Othello accepting an accusation by someone whom he has officially slighted and little knows, although the victims of the accusation are a newly wedded wife and an intimate friend. But Stoll argues, 'psychology, like law, is common sense, though art itself need not be' (p. 17). It is no solution to try to convert improbabilities into possibilities; rather we should follow Stoll in bearing in mind the word of 'Longinus', who writes: 'For grandeur produces ecstasy rather than persuasion in the hearer; and the combination of wonder and astonishment always proves superior to the merely persuasive and pleasant. This is because persuasion is on the whole something we can control, whereas amazement and wonder exert invincible power and force and get the better of every hearer.'[4] A spectator sitting in a theatre does not share the reaction of the critic whose analysis is contrived in the study. Drama, even if an average play is considerably longer than a Greek tragedy, must simplify and concentrate, and criticism is vitiated when, to quote Stoll, 'the play has been thought to be a psychological document, not primarily a play, a structure, both interdependent and independent, the parts mutually, and sufficiently, supporting and explaining each other; and the characters have been taken for the separable copies of reality' (p. 48). In *Othello*, in *Macbeth*, and in *Hamlet* 'it is upon an emotional situation, indeed, not a psychological problem (or even the avoidance of it) that . . . the dramatist throughout the play focuses his, and consequently our, attention' (p. 125). Sophocles' Oedipus may be able to solve the riddle of the Sphinx, a mystery which has all others baffled, but the hero of the *Oedipus Tyrannus* cannot see the truth about himself even when others can. Yet this is what makes the play so gripping, especially when we recall Apollo's instruction, 'know thyself'. Once we start being bothered by what, by the standard of absolute realism, is a remarkable coincidence, the fact that the servant who exposed the infant Oedipus is also the solitary survivor from the party of Laius after the clash between Oedipus and Laius at the crossroads, or we start speculating that Iocaste must have realized that she was marrying her own son because Oedipus was of exactly the right age, and, moreover, would have limped, we have long since ceased being critics of literature.

In Greek drama characters may change their mind or be persuaded by another with surprising rapidity, but this happens so that an already existing story may proceed with the minimum of fuss or hindrance, however much violence such a change of mind does to what we conceive to be a subtle delineation of character. It is no answer to dredge up 'evidence' in a desperate effort to show that the dramatist meant us to detect, too often with a microscope, earlier in the play signs which prepare the way for an abrupt conversion. In the *Antigone* the prophet Teiresias leaves the stage and Creon suddenly succumbs, appeals to the chorus for advice and with a spectacular *volte-face* authorizes the release of Antigone and the burial of Polyneices (verses 1091ff.). We are left breathless and the nineteenth-century critic like Jebb is driven to identify earlier in the play 'occasional glimpses of an uneasy conscience' on the part of the ruler of Thebes, actually citing verses 889f. and 1040.[5] But would an audience be acutely conscious of Creon's sudden reversal of attitude, and if it were, could it possibly recall 'hints' so scattered and so sparse? The most celebrated example of change of mind in the extant productions of Aeschylus is offered by Agamemnon's decision to enter his palace treading over the purple 'carpet'; the fact that Fraenkel was able to question the orthodox interpretation of Agamemnon's behaviour suggests that here again we are faced with a change of mind which is none too clearly motivated or related to characterization.[6] I must admit to having much sympathy with the opinion of Dawe who says of this incident, 'I believe that Agamemnon surrenders not because his character is especially chivalrous, or especially arrogant, but only because it was dramatically necessary that he should do so'.[7] Some changes of mind may be easier for us to accept and understand than others. Euripides' *Iphigenia in Aulis* opens with Agamemnon in the process of reversing a decision. He relates how, when Calchas broke the news that Iphigenia must be sacrificed if the Greeks were to be able to sail to Troy, he was persuaded by Menelaus to write home asking that his daughter be sent to Aulis, ostensibly as the bride of Achilles. Now he writes a second letter cancelling his instruction, but this letter is intercepted and read by Menelaus, who soundly abuses his brother for his change of mind. Yet later in the play Menelaus bursts in once more, this time to say that he has thought the matter over and sees Agamemnon's point of view (verses 480ff.)—he has also changed his mind and has changed it because of his affection for Agamemnon. Love of a father for his daughter and love of a brother for his brother explain this succession of events, but there is a further change of mind before the drama closes, and this last example is surely bewildering: having learned of her proposed death, Iphigenia implores her father and even the baby Orestes is held up as a speechless suppliant. The dilemma is resolved for Agamemnon by Iphigenia herself, however: although she had previously said that it is better to live ignominiously than to die nobly (verse 1252), she later proclaims her readiness to die for Greece (verses 1368ff.); her own death, it appears, is slight return for the honour of setting Greece free from barbarian threat. Referring to the example offered by Iphigenia, Aristotle remarks, and remarks justly, 'the girl who pleads for her life is quite different from the later one' (*Poetics* 1454a 32–33), and Lucas comments on Aristotle's criticism thus: 'It is true enought that Iphigeneia as suppliant is quite unlike her later self. In view of what passes between Clytemnestra and Achilles in her presence the transformation is by no means inexplicable, but *Euripides does nothing to explain it* (my own italics), and A.'s criticism is not so insensitive as is sometimes suggested. *In fact the economy of the play allows no scope for the development of Iphigeneia's character.*'[8]

New Comedy is no less at fault, though we profess to see in Menander a more naturalistic representation of life. Note, for example, the ease with which Sostratus in the *Dyskolos* convinces Gorgias that his intentions towards the latter's sister are strictly honourable (verses 302ff. and 315ff.). So abrupt a change of attitude on the part of Gorgias, the very sudden shedding of his earlier suspicions, is not to be referred to the plausibility of the young townsman or to the essential affability of Gorgias or to the playwright's desire to make the strongest possible contrast with the surliness of Cnemon (see verses 249–54), but rather to Menander's need to stimulate action in a comedy of considerable brevity, and a brevity which is the more striking if we exclude the farcical party which occupies so much of the fifth act. Equally abrupt, of course, is Gorgias' acquiescence in marriage to Sostratus' sister: in his note on verse 841 Handley attempts to explain so sudden a change of heart, but then adds 'but one suspects also that the poet has extracted all he wishes from the situation, and sees no cause to develop it with a further display of reluctance or a more fulsome assent'.[9] No character in any play is conceived with an absolute realism: some dramatic traditions aspire to more realism in the presentation of their *dramatis personae* than others, but these do not include Greek drama. The text of a Greek tragedy need not represent the case for or against any of the characters who appear in that play. It is folly, for example, to expect Sophocles in the *Oedipus Tyrannus* to justify Oedipus' act of self-mutilation. If, while driving my car, I were to run over and kill a child, or even worse, two people, say, my mother and father, I should probably wish never to drive again, however impeccable my driving and however stupid the behaviour of the victims. Some deeds are so appalling that they produce an extreme reaction irrespective of personal responsibility for their commission. To argue that Oedipus and Iocasta deserve their terrible fates on the grounds that both must have realized that the queen was marrying her own son, for Oedipus would have limped and the difference in their respective ages supported the prediction of the oracle, to argue along these or similar lines is absurd nonsense, and yet such an opinion has been advanced and is still maintained.[10]

But how are we to understand the Greek tragedian's treatment of those personages who appear in his play, and what relevance has his treatment of them to the question of the type of acting to be associated with the Greek theatre? Dale has been constructive no less than destructive in her criticism. Discussing attempts to penetrate the 'characters' of Admetus and Alcestis in her edition of Euripides' *Alcestis*, this scholar makes her views clear: 'The root of the trouble is, I think, our inveterate modern habit of regarding a drama almost exclusively in terms of its characters. The modern conception of the actor's function, with each actor concentrating on the "interpretation" of his single part, strongly reinforces this habit. It works quite well with modern drama, which is largely composed from the same point of view. It can be made to work with Shakespeare. But it will not work satisfactorily with Greek tragedy. Of course the Greek, like every serious drama, involves "characters", whose part in the action, and therefore, whose words, to some extent reflect their several natures. But in Greek tragedy their speeches, and the interplay of their dialogue, can rarely be interpreted as *primarily* or *consistently* expressive of their natures, and whenever we find ourselves trying to build up some elaborate or many-sided personality by *adding up* small touches gleaned from all parts of the play we can be pretty sure of being on the wrong lines. It usually means that we are not allowing enough for two considerations always very important to Greek dramatists, the trend of the action and the rhetoric of the situation.'[11] Later Dale develops her views, pointing out that 'in a well-constructed Euripidean tragedy what controls a succession of situations is not a firmly conceived unity of character but the shape of the whole action, and what determines the development and finesse of each situation is not a desire to paint in the details of a portrait-study but the rhetoric of the situation'. The rhetorical speech, delivered in the assembly, court of law, or on a public occasion, was as familiar to the Greek, who listened to the spoken word rather than read what was written, as the psychological novel is to us today. Whereas we have been conditioned to expect psychological depth to the characters presented in a play, the Greek looked for effective rhetoric, and, while effective rhetoric takes into account the personality of the speaker, it aims beyond all else to persuade. Dale appreciates that a modern actress might be embarassed when it comes to delivering the lines in which Alcestis tells Admetus that he can boast he possessed the noblest of wives and her children that they possessed the noblest of mothers (verses 323–25). These lines, she comments, are 'a pleader's peroration, not the spontaneous cry of a noble heart', and they presented no problem to 'the Greek actor, trained not in "interpretation" but in rhetorical performance, before an audience that expected nothing less'.[12] The rhetoric of the situation, according to Dale, is what Aristotle terms *dianoia*, the third of the six qualitative parts which the philosopher ascribes to tragedy (*Poetics* 1449b 21ff.), and 'the dianoia in a play *is* the eloquence of the personages, employed in putting their case on any occasion which requires it with all possible clarity and force. Their dianoia is the means by which an attitude of belief is produced in their hearers: they prove and disprove, exaggerate or gloss over, stir up emotions of pity, terror, indignation, calculated to influence belief.'[13] Here Dale elaborates on what Aristotle has to say when he refers to *dianoia* again later in the *Poetics* (1456a 36–b 2), and if Aristotle is brief, it is because *dianoia* falls within the province of rhetoric (1456a 34–36).

But how are we to describe, preferably in some measure of detail, style of acting determined by *dianoia* or the rhetoric of the situation? Before that question is posed, another must first be asked. To what extent can it be assumed that such a style of acting is typical of more than just the theatre of Euripides? What of Sophocles' actors and, for that matter, those who performed in the plays of Aeschylus? Dale, of course, does go back to Aristotle and in the *Poetics* the philosopher was thinking of all tragedy. The *Alcestis*, moreover, the play which first prompted Dale's discussion of *dianoia*, is the earliest extant work of Euripides and dates from 438 B.C.; in other words, it is hardly that much younger, if it is younger at all, than the earliest plays by Sophocles to have survived, and Dale does make reference to the *Antigone* and the *Ajax* in illustrating her argument. It has often been stated that Euripides' dramas are more rhetorical in character than those of Sophocles, and the plays of Aeschylus, with the exception of those making up the *Oresteia* trilogy, seem to be very different from the work of both Sophocles and Euripides. While the *Alcestis* was first produced in 438, the first public performance awarded Euripides was in

455, thirteen years after Sophocles had staged his first drama and won his first victory. Yet another date is significant: it was in 449 that the actors' competition for the protagonists was instituted, and, as was noted before (see our p. 44), a competition between actors implies some recognizable standard by which acting could be evaluated. Other developments date from the same period of time or slightly earlier: the third actor was introduced and poets ceased to act in their own plays, Sophocles reputedly because he possessed a weak voice.[14] A distinct style of acting, or perhaps it is better to say a distinct form of acting had presumably been evolved by the middle of the fifth century, and, if we allow a few years for this form of acting to have gained coherent shape, it seems that its evolution occurred when Sophocles had been producing plays for ten years or more, but that its evolution coincided with the beginnings of Euripides' professional career. It appears, then, that Euripides was born into a theatre whose acting was of this type, while Sophocles' craft was already mature, though still capable, of course, of adapting itself to meet new demands when acting acquired a 'professional' quality. That Sophocles in fact did develop his art and was conscious of such a development we know from a statement of the dramatist himself, preserved for us by Plutarch.[15] Effective speakers, however, existed before rhetoric became formalized and a Themistocles had no need of rules drawn up initially in Greek Sicily, nor also did Aeschylus. We commonly refer to the influence of the sophists on Greek drama: perhaps we should consider as well the influence of the dramatists on the sophistic movement. The evidence offered by the *Iliad* reveals that oratory was practised as early as Homer. The use of mythological parallels to support a case is also as old as the Homeric poems, though we associate the citation of mythological examples to justify a crime with the sophists. Yet already in the *Eumenides* of Aeschylus we find the Furies foxing, and infuriating, Apollo by quoting the example of Zeus as an instance of a person who, far from honouring a father, actually did violence to his parent (verses 640–41).

Although primarily a dramatic concept, Aristotle's *dianoia* is something affecting acting style, and it seems difficult to avoid a conclusion that it leads to a rhetorical style of acting, and so is yet another aspect of the supremacy of the spoken word in fifth-century Greece. Inasmuch as Elizabethan England was equally dominated by an essentially oral culture, we might expect to find that Elizabethan acting would be thought by some to exhibit the same rhetorical character, and this indeed is the case, a leading exponent of the theory being Joseph.[16] This scholar believes that Elizabethan acting was not formal,[17] and, in support of his opinion, cites the evidence offered by our handful of Pre-Restoration accounts of acting, evidence, as has been seen, which sadly does not exist for the Greek theatre in the fifth century B.C. But Joseph can go beyond a statement of belief, which actual evidence confirms. The sources available to him permit the observation that 'the excellent Elizabethan actor not only appeared as if he were the very man whom he represented, but showed in his acting everything that was to be commended in the delivery of an orator', and by orator is meant anybody skilled in the art of using language, and this also involved the use of voice, facial expression and gesture. There is no inconsistency in the view that acting was not formal but the arts of acting and oratory shared much in common, for the orator's devices were far from being divorced from an experience of real life and human behaviour. Rules might have been formulated for the orator, but these were rules based on the observation of people, and both orator and actor 'were expected to be natural and unaffected'.[18] Rather than being stereotyped, the delivery of the orator must be individualized, so that the personality of the orator and his actions form a match, or else the ability to carry conviction will soon be lost; the poor orator will over-play his hand just as much as the poor actor will. Certainly it is possible to point to evidence which suggests that oratory in fifth-century Athens was 'natural' both in general and in particular. Thus Aeschines in the fourth century refers to the practice of oratory a hundred years before: it would seem from his statement that Pericles, Themistocles and Aristides were so restrained that to speak with the arm outside the cloak, a standard procedure in the time of Aeschines, was thought to be ill-mannered and so avoided.[19] The departure from behaviour we may call natural appears to have begun with Cleon in the twenties of the fifth century B.C.: according to Aristotle in the *Constitution of Athens*, it was this politician who was the first to shout and hurl abuse from the tribunal and to address the people with his cloak tied up about him.[20] In Homer's *Iliad* Achilles strikes his thigh when addressing himself to Patroclus: to strike the thigh, the Roman Quintilian tells us, was a gesture reputed to have been introduced into oratory at Athens by the same Cleon.[21]

But perhaps we are making a case where there is no need to make a case. Dale's concern for the rhetoric of the situation is not unknown among students of Elizabethan drama, and one scholar, for instance, writes as follows: 'He (sc. Shakespeare) is concerned for a number of things besides character: ideas, words, wit. His speeches do not merely illustrate their speakers: what is said is more important than why it should be said. A joke is there for the joke's sake, and a wise word for its wisdom.'[22] I could end my quote here, and I would have shown, I think, an expert in another dramatic tradition making for the Elizabethan theatre the same point as Dale makes for the Greek theatre—what is said is more important than why it should be said. But if I continue with this quote from Bethell, the absurdity of too rigid a classification into what is 'formal' and what is 'natural' will also become apparent, for the quotation proceeds with these words: 'In a way, he is more natural than the naturalists. In ordinary conversation we ought, I suppose, to be able to trace every remark of our companion to its psychological source, to see it as reflecting his pride, or humility, or the fact that he was kicked by a horse in infancy. But in point of fact, most of us are content most of the time to be interested in what is said, for its own sake. The naturalistic playwright, however, is deliberately revealing character all the time; his interest in character has become morbid.'

We are wrong to draw an excessively rigid distinction between what is formal and what is natural. Habits change with time: we are horrified at the thought of a man spitting in anybody's face, father or no, and such an aversion in our own society to spitting in any form must be taken into account when we remark that Haemon is said to have spat in the face of his father Creon in Sophocles' *Antigone* (verse 1232). Distance affects behaviour no less than separation in time: Americans and continentals seem to shake hands whenever they meet, but an Englishman seldom greets his friend in this way. To do so would appear very formal to the Englishman. Society may be organized along more hierarchical lines than our own, and human behaviour in general may be more or less formalized. The Spartans were not the only Greeks whose life followed a set and rigid pattern. Modern life is as safe and certain as life in antiquity was precarious: the ancient Greek never knew from what quarter an enemy, and every stranger counted as an enemy, might strike next. Rules were, therefore, drawn up the universal recognition of which minimized, if it did not totally eliminate, the dangers surrounding man on every side. Thus the existence of rules has recently been noted in a study of the act of supplication among the Greeks, and the author of this study of the set procedure when one person appeals to another for help can refer to the rules of the game.[23] The chances of a head-on collision were less when the game of life followed a generally accepted set of rules. Greek life was 'formulaic': birth, marriage, death and much else among the Greeks were not haphazard events for the individual to manage as he wished; each adhered to a fixed procedure and was accompanied by the appropriate ceremonies, and the effect was to introduce and to maintain a measure of stability in a society which would otherwise have been faced with as many problems as events and which otherwise would have been strained to the point of constantly breaking down.[24] Modern man can afford to be much more free when it comes to human relationships.

Acting is always a conscious process, but the Greek or Elizabethan surely could remain in character, could identify himself with the part he was playing on the stage more readily than his modern counterpart, who, when he appears in a play by any of the Greek tragedians or by Shakespeare, is inevitably inhibited by the knowledge that he is performing in a 'classic' and that the interpretation of his role has been the subject of a critical discussion which has stretched back over the centuries. The speech a Greek or an Elizabethan actor was required to deliver might have been 'unrealistic', couched as it was in verse (but compare *Poetics* 1449a 24–28), but this does not mean that it could not be spoken naturally. Greek and Elizabethan plays were performed in the hours of daylight, but the setting might be at night, as it is when the *Agamemnon* opens; yet an actor can behave in day-light as if it were actually the night no less unnaturally than he can address another in verse, although real life is conducted in prose. The stage-building of the Greek theatre may serve as a temple or a palace, but the audience which sat watching the play did not reason 'this is the stage-building, but it is one of the conventions of our theatrical tradition that it may represent a temple or palace'. They were told by a character in the play that the structure located behind the stage was a palace, and it became a palace. The mechanical devices available to the dramatist—the crane by means of which a god might be introduced and the *eccyclema* to present on stage something which really happened off-stage out of the spectators' view—were crude. But yet again, when the *eccyclema* was trundled out on stage or whatever, the audience did not con-sciously think 'this happened inside because it is accommodated on the *eccyclema*, and the *eccyclema* is a conventional device which our play-wrights employ so as to bring before the audience what occurred off-stage'. What Joseph has said of the Elizabethan play is equally true of Greek drama: 'When the play succeeded, the audience imagined it as involving imaginary persons, incidents, and places which evoked a response as if they were really the things represented. It did not matter whether the imaginary was represented realistically or unrealistically, so long as it was accepted and treated as if it were not imaginary by the actors.'[25] At one point in the *Rhesus* the goddess Athene, conversing with Diomedes, notes the approach of Paris. Diomedes is eager to attack the Trojan prince, but Athene points out that Paris is not due to fall victim to Diomedes, who must go against Rhesus instead. Athene purposes to distract Paris taking on the guise of another deity, the goddess Aphrodite. Paris, she adds, although nearby knows nothing and has not heard what she has said (verses 627–41). Athene next proceeds to address Paris who believes her to be Aphrodite. However close on the stage to Athene Paris might be, he does not hear what the goddess says because Athene states that he has failed to hear her words; Paris thinks that Athene is Aphrodite without there being any need for Athene to adopt a disguise because Athene says that he will believe her to be Aphrodite. A passage such as this reveals the extent which an audience is prepared to accept what is told convincingly on the stage.

Not being subject to the physical limitations which restrict any production in a theatre, a film can be realistic to a degree denied a play, be it ancient or modern. But it is amazing how unquestioningly we accept the conventions of the cinema, failing to recognize that many of them are in fact conventions. In a film designed for the North American or British markets the characters in that film speak English, irrespective of their supposed nationality or the historical period to which they appear to belong. It is a convention, and a very convenient one, that the characters speak contemporary English, whether the film is set in Rome of the Caesars, Stuart England, or among the natives of the Polynesian islands. The same type of convention is also illustrated by Greek drama, though we do not, or do not generally, reckon it a convention simply because we are so familiar with it. In the Homeric *Hymn to Aphrodite*, when Aphrodite appears before Anchises, the goddess explains her ability to address the Trojan in his native tongue, though ostensibly a Phrygian princess, by stating that she had had a Trojan nurse and so learned Anchises' tongue as well as her own (verses 113–16). Of course, she is actually speaking in Greek! Thus an impression of reality is created which is no true reality, but the passage is remarkably convincing. The Thracians in the *Rhesus* would seem to need to be addressed in Thracian (see verses 294–97), but, like the Trojans also featured in the play, speak Greek when on stage. The choruses in Aeschylus' *Supplices* and Euripides' *Phoenissae* sing their songs in Greek but an impression is given that they are using their own non-Greek languages, in the former drama by what the chorus itself says (cf. verses 118–19 and 129–30; cf. also *Bacchae*, 1034), and in the latter drama by Iocasta referring to their 'Phoenician call' (verses 301–2; cf. also 679, 680 and 1301). When Euripides' Phrygian enters on the stage in the *Orestes*, he laments the ruin of Troy in 'barbarian cry' (verse 1385), employing, however, as you would expect, the Greek language. Aeschylus can exploit the fact that Cassandra is no Greek: in the *Agamemnon* Clytemnestra assumes that Cassandra's slowness to obey her new mistress may be the result of her not understanding Greek (verses 1035ff., and especially 1050–51 and 1060–61), but then Cassandra lets flow a veritable flood of words, and, if what she says is in any way confused, this is to be referred to her prophetic role and not to an imperfect knowledge and command of the Greek tongue.[26] The Persians in Aeschylus' play of that name converse in Greek, although the poet Timotheus, when composing on the same theme as Aeschylus and in a work which bears the same name as the play by the tragedian, presents us with a barbarian attempting to speak Greek (verses 162ff.). The *Persae* is the one extant play with a contemporary plot but all its characters are Persians and exotic in race by the standards of tragedy. In his *Acharnians* Aristophanes lets his Persian ambassador speak a line of 'Persian' and a line of pseudo-Greek (verses 100 and 104); later in the same comedy Aristophanes makes us laugh at the dialect of a man from Megara and a Boeotian (verses 729ff. and 860ff.). It is part of Orestes' plan in the *Choephori* that he should appear at the palace disguised as a stranger, and that he and Pylades should speak in the Phocian dialect of Greek (verses 560–64); in his first words to Clytemnestra Orestes declares himself to be from Phocis (verse 675), but it is not necessary that Aeschylus carry realism to the point of actually inflicting Phocian Greek on his Athenian audience, and Attic Greek is good enough for Orestes when the palace is reached (verses 653ff.). The failure to fulfil a detail in his plans elicits a long comment from Paley, a nineteenth-century editor of the poet, who speaks of 'tragic propriety' to explain away the apparent 'inconsistency', and further adds: 'it may be remarked also, that all which is really professed here is, that the two companions will *converse* in that patois, in order to gain admission by deceiving the doorkeepers. There is no pledge to address Clytemnestra or Aegisthus in a feigned dialect.' A logical explanation? Perhaps. But then no logical explanation is required: like a modern cinema audience the Greeks sitting in the Theatre of Dionysus accepted what was said, were carried along by the surge of the drama and were hardly likely to share Paley's confusion. The language employed in a film or a play is naturally the language understood by the audience; it is inevitable that this is so and its very inevitability means that it is seldom noticed or listed in a catalogue of typical conventions.

More examples could be discussed but these would merely confirm that we fail to recognize as essentially unrealistic those conventions which Greek drama and modern forms of the dramatist's art share in common. The musical film offers an example of a mixture of dialogue and song, and the tendency during the last twenty-five years has been to produce musical films whose plots have been anything other than romantic: a Pacific island threatened by Japanese invasion or a Nazi-dominated Europe, for instance, have been the setting of highly successful musicals. A character in such a production can alternate between conversation and lyric outburst without an average member of the audience detecting anything incongruous in the action and behaviour of that character. The film is 'realistic' enough, as is Greek drama, for the reason given by Joseph which I have already quoted. Operatic performance is no less suggestive. Indeed a comparison with opera has been skilfully deployed by L. H. G. Greenwood in his discussion of realism and Greek tragedy.[27] It was Greenwood who identified as a convention of Greek tragedy what he called the 'lyric-iambic sequence'. This scholar noted as a regular feature of Greek plays a sequence in which a character sings lyric lines and then delivers a monologue or engages in a dialogue in iambic verses without the change from lyric to iambic advancing the action of the drama in any way: 'In such cases, spoken verse is resumed only to be the vehicle of a further response or reaction of the person concerned to the same situation as before; the whole episode may even end with no development in the action of the play. This further response or reaction is, on the whole and as a rule, more rational and intellectual, less purely emotional, than that already expressed in the lyrical passage: it tells us more of what the speaker thinks, less of what he feels. But this is all that is new: there are no fresh events.' Greenwood stresses the folly of seeing any profound 'psychological' significance when the sequence is so regular: we must not assume that a character in a play 'pulls him or herself together' because lyric outburst gives way to seemingly more restrained iambics. Greenwood can afford to be dogmatic for a very simple reason, the reverse sequence, from iambic verses to lyric, does not occur: 'The change of tone is always from the more agitated to the more tranquil, from the more emotional to the more rational: never in the other direction.' The lyric-iambic sequence is a convention of Greek tragedy and does not suggest 'with some degree of realism, an actual and corresponding change of mental attitude in the speaker'. A comparison with eighteenth-century and early nineteenth-century oratorio and opera is instructive, for here a similar convention may be detected in the alternation of recitative and aria, though in this case the sequence is reversed, recitative corresponding to spoken iambics and aria to sung lyric.

Joseph is in the fortunate position of being able to refer to rhetorical handbooks, and can, therefore, discuss in some measure of detail the rhetorical style of acting practised by the Elizabethans. We have no evidence from antiquity of this kind to which reference may be made earlier in date than the Roman Quintilian, and evidence from the first century A.D. is of dubious relevance. A rhetorical style of acting need not prevent quite vigorous action on the stage, and indeed it is clear, as we have seen in an earlier chapter, than such action did occur in Greek drama. At the same time one would not expect continuous bustle on the part of the actors. Time is consumed if actors bustle about and again, if less obviously so, if heavy and frequent pauses punctuate the dialogue. Quintilian recommends a pause for thought by the orator before he addresses the court, quoting the example offered by Odysseus in the *Iliad*.[28] In this passage Homer contrasts the oratorical style of Menelaus and Odysseus: Menelaus is said to speak rapidly (*Iliad* iii. 213), and, if Odysseus paused, this was only before he began his speech, for once under way his words 'came drifting down like the winter snows' (verse 222), a simile which presumably points a contrast with the few words said to be characteristic of Menelaus (verse 214), but a simile which hardly suggests much in the way of a pause between words or sentences. A person who declaims today, whether politician or actor, certainly speaks with deliberation and frequent resort to pauses, but it would be most unwise to assume that such a technique is common to all speakers at all periods of time and in all places. Oral literature still flourishes in modern Africa, and this literature includes the panegyric or praise poem.[29] In fact it has been said that 'in its specialized form panegyric is *the* type for court poetry and is one of the most developed and elaborate poetic genres in Africa'.[30] Best known is the praise poetry of the Southern Bantu, poetry which incorporates a narrative element (for example, the description of battles and hunts) but the general treatment of which is dramatic and panegyric. We know something of the way in which such poems are delivered and what we know is perhaps surprising: 'There seems to be general agreement that praise poems are delivered much faster, and in a higher tone, than ordinary prose utterances. The reciter pours forth the praises with few pauses for breath and at the top of his voice. Often there is a growing excitement and dramatic gestures are made as the poem proceeds. Grant describes a well-known Zulu praiser whom he heard in the 1920s. As the poet recited, he worked himself up to a high pitch of fervour, his face was uplifted, and his voice became loud and strong. The shield and stick that he carried were, from time to time, suddenly raised and shaken, and his gestures became more frequent and dramatic, so that he would suddenly leap in the air or crouch with glaring eyes while praises poured from his lips— until at last he stopped exhausted.'[31] To compare Bantu poets and Greek actors is absurd, especially now when it is no longer fashionable to equate the techniques of Yugoslav *guslar* and Homer, but, if it proves nothing else, the description quoted above reveals that a dogmatic belief that a speaker must declaim slowly, frequently stopping to draw breath and also to allow his audience to savour the force of the words, is impossible.

   Satyrus is the source of a tradition that Sophocles choked himself to death while reading, obviously aloud, his *Antigone*: delivering a passage which permitted no pause for breath, and 'straining to excess voice with voice', he gave up his life.[32] Is this just a comment on the poet's celebrated weakness of voice? Probably so. But 'straining voice with voice' suggests dialogue between a pair of characters, and stichomythia surely demands a rapid exchange between the actors, as does also the trochaic tetrameter in the later plays of Euripides; this is the metre employed, for instance, when Xuthus in the *Ion* comes out from the oracle and greets Ion as his son (verses 510–65): the exuberance of Xuthus is matched by Ion's embarrassment, and the excitement engendered by this meeting is marked by a whole succession of lines divided between the two actors with the one constantly interrupting the other (verses 530–62). But we can, I think, do little more in our present state of knowledge than to emphasize that the ponderous delivery thought appropriate to the modern actor when performing in a Greek or Shakespearean play is no guide to the form of delivery practised when these plays were contemporary productions and an actor had no idea that he was appearing in a drama destined to be considered a 'classic' of European drama. An element of formality in delivery, I would concede, is suggested by a pattern of presentation which occurs time and time again in Greek tragedy: a long speech is delivered in turn by each of two characters present on the stage, and the two speeches are not continuous, one following immediately upon the other, but are separated by two lines from the chorus. Such a pattern implies that each speaker stands apart on his own side of the stage, and that the brief intervention on the part of the chorus allows the audience to turn its attention from the first to the second speaker while also causing the end of one speech and the beginning of another to be clearly marked. Formal such an arrangement may be, but it is a very slight and a particular degree of formal presentation, serving the special purpose of separating two lengthy speeches.

One further misconception remains to be corrected before our discussion of actors and acting is concluded. Too often it is taken for granted that the fifth century B.C. was an age when the leading figure was the playwright, but that this position was surrendered to the actor in the next century. There are reasons for such an assumption: Aeschylus, Sophocles and Euripides lived and worked and wrote in the fifth century, whereas the dominant literary figures in the fourth century, if we exclude the writers of comedy, are Plato the philosopher and Isocrates the rhetorician, both of whom saw prose as usurping what before had been the function of poetry. In the fourth century the three great dramatists became classic figures and revivals of their plays were staged at the City Dionysia. At first sight creative ability appears to have given way to criticism of the type exemplified by the *Poetics*, whose author, after all, does tell us that in his day actors had more power than had the playwrights.[33] The result is that we draw a sharp and exclusive distinction between the Greek theatre in the fifth and in the fourth century, typifying one as a dramatist's theatre and the other as an actor's theatre, deploring, of course, the latter. This distinction is too facile: there were famous actors in the fifth century, and the introduction of a competition between them in 449 B.C. is some indication of their considerable fame at this time. Actors were celebrated and they achieved celebrity through the deployment of their voices. The audience came wishing to hear rather than to see, and the dramatic tradition, as well as the actual theatre, was ideally suited to meet the wishes of the spectators. Vitruvius wrote on architecture at the time of the late Roman Republic and early Empire and so may offer evidence no more valid than that supplied by the words of Quintilian, but there is one remarkable feature in his instructions for the would-be theatre architect which is well worth our noting.[34] While his treatise includes chapters on harmony, sounding vessels in the theatre and acoustics, he passes only one remark which suggests a concern with the spectators' ability to see what was taking place on the stage; in his chapter on the plan of the theatre he stipulates that the stage is not to be more than five feet in height, since senators sit in the orchestra of the Roman theatre and these would otherwise be unable to see the gestures of all the actors (v. 6. 2). Apart from this solitary remark he is bothered only that the audience's hearing be unimpeded, and advice to achieve this end is offered freely throughout his discussion of the theatre. The public theatres of Elizabethan England were not unlike the ancient theatre in their general design, but it is only recently that the case for their having been influenced by the theatre as described by Vitruvius has been systematically and convincingly put.[35] In the course of presenting this case Yates makes and re-makes a point which has been central to my own study, and it is for this reason that I close my discussion of actors and acting with three quotations from Yates, for the second and third do more than repeat the first; they also amplify it. 'The Shakespearean type of theatre was a predominantly aural theatre, suited to be the vehicle of a great poetic drama, to be a vast sounding box in which nothing interrupted the resonance of the words spoken on the stage from reaching every part of the theatre.' 'This theatre was pre-eminently an aural theatre, like the ancient theatre, placing the main emphasis on the words spoken on the stage and their audibility.' 'It preserved the most important aspects of the ancient theatre, its cosmic and therefore religious implications, its acoustic properties and emphasis on the voice, its enhancement of poetry and the spoken words as the main means of communication between actors and audience. And by their very size, their capacity for holding large numbers, the English theatres were public theatres in the ancient sense.'[36] This final reference to a huge seating capacity and the description 'public theatres' will remind my readers of what was said in the first chapter of this study. My next chapter will also serve to stimulate a recollection of the argument with which my book opened.

NOTES

1 *Poetics* 1450a 22.
2 *Collected Papers*, p. 273. For a general discussion of characterization in Greek drama, see G. H. Gellie, *Journal of the Australasian Universities Language and Literature Association* 20 (1963), pp. 241–55.
3 E. E. Stoll, *Art and Artifice in Shakespeare* (Cambridge, 1933); see also *The Review of English Studies* 19 (1943), pp. 25–32. Compare chapter VI 'The question of characterisation' in Bradbrook, *Elizabethan Stage Conditions* (Cambridge, 1932); it will be seen from the note prefacing the second impression of this book that Bradbrook's views remain constant thirty years later. Similarly worth consulting is the work of another English specialist, A. J. A. Waldock, *Sophocles, the Dramatist* (Cambridge, 1951), who writes on the 'documentary fallacy', pp. 11–24.
4 *On Sublimity* i. 4, as translated by D. A. Russell in *Ancient Literary Criticism, the Principal Texts in New Translations*, p. 462.
5 R. C. Jebb, *Sophocles, Antigone* (Cambridge,[2] 1891), pp. xv-xvi.
6 See Eduard Fraenkel's note on verse 811 of the *Agamemnon* in his edition of that play (Oxford, 1950).
7 R. D. Dawe, *Proceedings of the Cambridge Philological Association* 189 (1963), p. 50. Discussion of Agamemnon's motive and its relevance to Aeschylean characterization continues: see, most recently, Michael Simpson, *La Parola del Passato* 137 (1971), pp. 94–101, and P. E. Easterling, *Greece and Rome* 20 (1973), pp. 3–19.
8 D. W. Lucas, *Aristotle, Poetics* (Oxford, 1968), note on 1454a 32.
9 E. W. Handley, *The Dyskolos of Menander* (London, 1965).
10 Notoriously by Philip Vellacott, *Sophocles and Oedipus* (London, 1971), but compare Dodds, *Greece and Rome* 13 (1966), pp. 37ff. (=*The Ancient Concept of Progress and Other Essays on Greek Literature and Belief* [Oxford, 1973], pp. 64–77), and Hugh Lloyd-Jones, *The Justice of Zeus* (Berkeley, 1971), pp. 104ff.
11 *Euripides, Alcestis* (Oxford, 1954), pp. xxiv-xxv.
12 Ibid. pp. xxvii and xxviii.
13 *Collected Papers*, p. 149.
14 *Vit. Soph.* 4.
15 *Moralia* 79 B.
16 *Elizabethan Acting.* pp. 1ff. A convenient summary of the main points made by Joseph is offered by this same author's book, *The Tragic Actor* (London, 1959), pp. 1–27.
17 Compare Joseph on Harbage, ibid. p. 106.
18 Ibid. pp. 5 and 7.
19 Aeschines, *Timarchus* 25–26.
20 *Ath. Pol.* 28, 3.
21 *Iliad* xvi. 125 and Quin. xi. 3. 123.
22 S. L. Bethell, *Shakespeare and the Popular Dramatic Tradition* (London/New York, 1944), p. 79.
23 John Gould, *Journal of Hellenic Studies* 93 (1973), pp. 74–103.
24 Cf. J. A. Notopoulos, *Harvard Studies in Classical Philology* 68 (1964), pp. 50–51 and 53–54.
25 Op. cit. p. 109.
26 Cf. Fraenkel's comment (see note 6) on verse 1061.
27 *Aspects of Euripidean Tragedy* (Cambridge, 1953), pp. 132–39.
28 Quin. xi. 3. 157ff.
29 For details see Ruth Finnegan, *Oral Literature in Africa* (Oxford, 1970).
30 Ibid. pp. 111ff. and, on the praise poetry of the Southern Bantu, pp. 121ff.
31 Ibid. pp. 137–38.
32 *Vit. Soph.* 14.
33 *Rhet.* 1403b 33.
34 *De Architectura* v. 3–8.
35 F. A. Yates, *Theatre of the World* (London, 1969).
36 Ibid. pp. 124, 128 and 129.

Drama and Social Values

WHILE discussing acting and actors we saw that certain restrictions must be taken into account when we consider the type and degree of characterization allowed the Greek tragedian. A further restriction must now be noted, and this restriction will take us back to the opening chapter and our discussion of the audience which attended the first productions of the plays of Aeschylus, Sophocles and Euripides. It will be recalled that there it was argued that a dramatist competing for the first prize at the City Dionysia would not inflict upon the spectators profound philosophy but would express, through his characters, sentiments, prejudices and ideas shared by the audience (see our pp. 3–4). In other words, persons in a play will reflect the values of contemporary society, and such values will not necessarily coincide with those we hold dear today, two and a half millennia later. Fifth-century Greeks neither knew the tenets of Christianity as exemplified by the Sermon on the Mount nor had they experienced an equivalent of our industrial, technological revolution. To be understood fully, Greek drama needs to be put in its social as well as in its theatrical context, but this few have been concerned to do. What Harbage has said of Shakespeare's plays is equally true of fifth-century drama: 'Shakespeare's plays would not have been enjoyed if they had offended the moral and religious sentiments prevailing in the audience for which they were designed. A basic conformity with the current system of values must be assumed.'[1]

An example taken from Homer's *Odyssey* will reveal the extent of the gulf which divides our own concept of social and moral values from that typical of the Greeks throughout classical antiquity. In the thirteenth book of that poem Odysseus eventually reaches the island of Ithaca. Waking up in his native land, he fails to recognize where he has been left by the Phaeacians (verses 187ff.). He is approached, however, by the goddess Athene, disguised as a young man, and the pair exchange words. Told that he is actually in Ithaca, Odysseus relates the first of a series of long, lying stories, claiming to be a Cretan forced to take flight after he has killed a son of Idomeneus (verses 256ff.). Nothing, it seems, is more useful to men than a prudent distrust (cf. Euripides, *Helen* 1617–18), and this principle is adopted by the hero of the *Odyssey*. Odysseus is anxious to win the sympathy and help of his new acquaintance, and it seems reasonable to assume that this fiction is carefully contrived to achieve just that. Yet the story he tells would scarcely win the ungrudging approval of a modern listener: Odysseus states that he served at Troy but with an independent command and not under the command of Idomeneus; on his return to Crete Idomeneus' son, Orsilochus, wanted to deprive him of all the booty for which he had laboured so long and hard. Odysseus' response was violent: he killed Orsilochus, having ambushed him at night with the aid of a companion (verses 267–70). Chivalry was no consideration here, and the killing, from an ambush, at night, and with assistance, seems particularly sordid and is prompted by a crude desire for revenge, on both sides, which is no less sordid. Indeed in Euripides' *Rhesus*, the Thracian prince whose name supplies the play with its title denounces Odysseus when told by Hector of Odysseus' liking for the ambush, declaring that no true man kills his enemy by stealth but goes to meet him face to face (verses 510–11). Yet the threat with which he follows this comment and his own death slightly later render these words an empty boast. But to return to the *Odyssey*, if one of us were to find himself in a comparable situation, newly arrived home after an absence of twenty years and with no inkling of what had happened at home during that period of time, would he introduce himself to a stranger with so unflattering a story? Hardly. But to a Greek what is achieved, the results of action, is something all important, having absolute priority, whereas the means which led to the results count for much less. Orsilochus was dead, and Odysseus had extracted revenge for the attempt made to strip him of his legitimate spoils. At one point in Euripides' *Hippolytus* the Nurse ruefully remarks, 'if I had been successful, I would have been reckoned wise' (verse 700); Odysseus had been successful, and so could lay claim to a reputation for wisdom. Motive and means are irrelevant in a society where personal prestige and material achievement rank high, and any such society must run the risk of denying to its dramatists what we regard as a crucial element in the depiction of character. For us it is the inward debate as a character tries to decide upon his course of action, assessing his motives as much as his opportunities, which enables the dramatist to display his talent for characterization. The slight importance attached to motivation in Greek society appears to eliminate the prime material available to the dramatist when he wishes to develop 'character'.

Homer composed his epics some three hundred years before Aeschylus, Sophocles and Euripides wrote for the stage, and attitudes change in time, especially in a century like the fifth century B.C., which opens with the Greeks in conflict with the Persians, continues with the formation of an Athenian empire, and closes with the ancient equivalent of our two World Wars. Herodotus during that century revealed that customs varied from people to people, and the human behaviour, therefore, was not based on an absolute standard; the sophists, travelling from city to city, spread new ideas throughout the Greek world; as it dragged on for twenty-seven years and spread from mainland Greece to Sicily in the West and to Asia Minor in the East, the Peloponnesian War persuaded both sides to take action which became increasingly more repressive. By the turn of the century Athens was smashed and Sparta triumphant, but the rest of Greece found that it had lost one master only to acquire another and that its new master showed little enthusiasm for promoting the freedom of others. Motives have now become important, and so a contrast may be drawn between the two Oedipus plays by Sophocles: 'in the *Oedipus Tyrannus* Oedipus' intentions and motives are irrelevant, but in the *Oedipus at Colonus* they are of great importance.'2 Yet change in attitude must wait until the end of the fifth century before it becomes significant, and an earlier play by Sophocles, his *Trachiniae*, includes a passage which echoes the sentiments and attitude of mind which we noted in our extract from the thirteenth book of the *Odyssey*. It offers another example of a story of insult, retaliation and violent death, although it also features an important qualification.

In this play Lichas explains how Heracles was obliged to spend a year in the service of the barbarian queen Omphale (verses 248ff.); stung by such a disgrace he swore an oath to avenge himself by enslaving in turn the man who was responsible and that man's family (verses 254–57). The culprit was Eurytus, a person who had welcomed Heracles into his house as a friend of long standing but had then insulted his guest, claiming superiority for his sons in the use of bow and arrows, before finally, in his drunkeness, driving Heracles from the house. Heracles retaliated by killing Iphitus, the son of Eurytus, when he came to Tiryns, hurling him down from a height when caught unawares. The murder of Iphitus was punished by Zeus, who enslaved the hero to Omphale (verses 260–76). But why was Zeus so furious at the death of Iphitus that he punished his son? It was not because of what we would regard as the obvious reason, the simple act of killing. He did not tolerate it, Lichas says, because Iphitus alone of men Heracles killed 'by guile' (verses 277–78). The comment is then expanded: 'if Heracles had avenged himself openly, Zeus would have pardoned him for a just attempt' (verses 278–79). The gods, it seems, do not care for *hybris* (verse 280), but it was the manner of Iphitus' death and not the death itself which incurred the anger of Zeus. Heracles had been the guest of Eurytus and an old friend; he was treated abominably by his host and Eurytus' drunkenness was no excuse. Retaliation is as valid a principle for Heracles as it was for Odysseus or as it was for Orsilochus. Odysseus insulted Idomeneus by not serving under him at Troy; the son of Idomeneus sought revenge by trying to seize the booty; Odysseus killed Orsilochus and was forced to flee Crete to avoid retaliation from the relatives of the dead man. Eurytus insulted and maltreated

Heracles; the hero killed Iphitus, and Zeus, angered by the fact that Heracles chose to kill Iphitus by guile, sold Heracles into slavery; Heracles destroyed the city of Eurytus and captured its women. Violence in itself is accepted as a norm of human behaviour, and there is no Sermon on the Mount to teach us that two wrongs do not add up to a right. No law, we read in Euripides' *Ion*, stands in the way when one wants to do harm to an enemy (verses 1046–47). We may find such brutality distressing, but the Greeks did not. War to us is appalling and never more so than today; war offered the Greek a chance to display his manhood. In one sense the Greek attitude is more 'realistic', since it accepts human nature for what it is. Earlier in the *Trachiniae* the messenger tells Deianeira that, on hearing Lichas' proclamation that Heracles was returning home safe and victorious, he dashed away to be the first to announce the good news to the queen that he might gain profit and gratitude from Deianeira (verses 189–91). 'The messenger is at all events abundantly candid in confessing his scurvy motive', says a note attached to a nineteenth-century translation of Sophocles, but such frankness is typical of messengers in Greek tragedy (e.g. *Oedipus Tyrannus*, 1005–6) and the pursuit of gain is not to be thought disreputable, for gain enhances a man's prestige. Being devoid of inhibitions and not subject to the pangs of moral conscience, the Greek could adopt what might be described as a 'healthy' attitude towards life and its problems. Revenge is not fashionable today, though it provided both the Greek and the Elizabethan playwright with much of his material.

A seemingly moral note may be struck in the *Odyssey*, as it is, for example, after Odysseus has killed off the suitors: the aged Eurycleia enters the hall and sees the dead bodies; any open rejoicing on her part is quickly suppressed by Odysseus, who informs his servant that it is not holy to gloat over the dead; the suitors, he says, have fallen victim to the gods and the reason is their wicked deeds (*Od.* xxii. 411–16). Odysseus spares Phemius and Medon, telling the latter that he may inform another that a good deed is much better than an evil deed (verses 373-74), yet the unfaithful servants are slaughtered, a particularly vicious punishment being inflicted on Melanthius (verses 475–77). In spite of the occasional note which suggests ethical standards we would applaud, it is a hard world, and we must not expect anything good from one who has suffered because of us, a lesson which Deianeira accepts in the course of the *Trachiniae* (verses 707ff.). The critic builds up a picture of Deianeira, seeing her as a noble, loving wife, but is devastated when she states that you will never fall into shame if it is in the dark that you do what is shameful (verses 596–97). This is a sentiment reminiscent of a comment passed by Euripides' Nurse in the *Hippolytus*, when it is pointed out

that no one really minds provided there is no open scandal (cf. verses
462–66):

> Tell me, how many
> of the wise ones of the earth do you suppose
> see with averted eyes their wives turned faithless;
> how many erring sons have father helped
> with secret loves? It is the wise man's part
> to leave in darkness everything that is ugly.[3]

But the remark does not bother us in the *Hippolytus*, for the Nurse is
considered to have no moral scruples, especially if the well-being of
Phaedra is threatened, and, after all, this is Euripides writing, not Sophocles. Cynicism, however, must be distinguished from what is rather
a realistic, hard-headed appraisal of a situation, and to be realistic in
terms of values, as we have been seeing, is typically Greek, and certainly
not an attitude of mind solely reserved for characters in Euripidean
drama. The same conviction, that a shameful deed, when kept concealed
is no source of shame, has been recognized among the inhabitants of
a Greek mountain village today: 'there is a very significant sense in
which it is considered more important to be seen to be honourable than
it is actually to be so . . . Although theoretically it is the reality of honour
that is considered to be fundamental to personality, it is in practice the
appearance of honour which is in this society the vital arbitrator of
behaviour.'[4]

In the *Choephori* of Aeschylus Orestes given his reasons for avenging
the death of his father Agamemnon, and only the first two of these are
acceptable by the standard of our moral values, the command of heaven
and great grief for his parent; he has a third incentive as well, his lack of
substance, disinherited as he is (verses 299–301). In its reply the chorus
imagine Dike crying out aloud as she extracts what is owed: for a word
of enmity let a word of enmity, for a murderous blow let a murderous
blow be paid; that the doer suffers is a time-hallowed saying (verses
309–14). Where murder is in question, there is more than proverbial
wisdom to guide us; it is a law that blood demands blood (verses 400–4).
Sophocles' Orestes is no more scrupulous. At the beginning of the *Electra*
he instructs the *paidagogos* as to what action he is to take; he tells his
servant to report his own false death, adding an oath (verses 47–48).
Deception is forgivable but is an oath either necessary or justifiable?
Orestes explains his own attitude quite openly: 'I consider no statement
bad if attended by profit' (verse 61). This is very much the approach of
Odysseus in the *Philoctetes*, but it is embarrassing not to have an Orestes
who is as much a stickler for the truth as Neoptolemus is in that play
(cf. verses 86–95). Sophocles' Electra is also concerned for material

rewards, as she reveals later in the *Electra* when she attempts to secure the support of Chrysothemis (verses 959–85). She points out to her sister how Chrysothemis has been deprived of her father's wealth and the expectation of marriage; in joining Electra the sister will stand to gain the approval of her dead father and her brother, freedom, a worthy marriage and general praise, the last of these advantages being heavily stressed as Electra describes the glorious reputation that they will acquire both while alive and when dead. She finishes her appeal by asking her sister to recognize that it is shameful for the nobly born to live shamefully (verse 989). Reputation is the strongest incentive to action and success a guarantee of reputation, as Lichas notes in the *Trachiniae* (verses 230–31); the only option open to Deianeira when her reputation is forfeit is suicide (verses 719–22).

Electra is a woman, not a man, says Chrysothemis when she rejects Electra's arguments, and her strength does not match that of her opponents (verses 997–98). Such a statement, reinforced by the use of the Greek verb *phuein* ('to be disposed by nature'; compare, for example, *Philoctetes*, 88), reveals how the Greeks thought of women as having a disposition which was quite distinct from the *physis* or disposition/nature of men, and how, therefore the kind of behaviour expected of a woman was different from what was considered appropriate behaviour for a man. Thus, when Aristotle in the *Poetics* speaks of the characters represented being 'suitable' (1454a 22–24), he remarks, 'for example, the character represented is brave, but it is not suitable for a woman to be brave or clever in this way'. If so many of the really memorable characters in Greek tragedy are women, Clytemnestra, Electra, Antigone, Medea and Phaedra, we can see why a female character might offer the playwright the maximum scope for dramatic impact; let a woman turn her back on what were thought the virtues appropriate for a woman and attempt to usurp what was properly man's function, and we are likely to find a situation fraught with excitement. The impact of such a character in the Greek theatre before an audience which did not believe in the 'equality' of the sexes or that a woman was entitled to a life and career of her own must have been overwhelming. But there is more to it than a simple belief that women were different and that women were inferior. Women also, in the eyes of the Greek male, were fundamentally bad and the sexual act another trap for men. Confirmation was offered by the earliest 'history', the farthest reaches of the mythological past. In his *Theogony* the poet Hesiod relates how the first woman, Pandora, was sent down from heaven by Zeus in retaliation for the theft of fire by Prometheus (verses 570ff.). Insidiously attractive, Pandora was the source of a man's tribulations, since a very feminine curiosity caused her to open the jar which released evils upon the world (cf. *Works and Days*, 90ff.). And how was Uranus, the first king of heaven, displaced by his son Cronus? This story Hesiod also tells in the *Theogony*: Cronus ambushed and castrated Uranus (verses 154ff.). The plot was engineered by a female, Gaia, the wife of Uranus and the mother of Cronus, who provided her son with both a weapon and the occasion, and the occasion was when Uranus made love with Gaia (verses 176–78). Yet again the principle of retaliation applied, since Gaia claimed, and her words were repeated by Cronus, that Uranus was the first to do outrage (verses 166 and 172).

Deianeira was not a woman who murdered her husband or children, or a woman who defied the edicts of the ruler of the state, or a woman who made advances to her step-son. She was herself threatened by the amorous interest of the river-god Achelous, but her rescue was affected by Heracles. In relating at the beginning of the *Trachiniae* the story of the events which led up to her marriage to Heracles (verses 1ff.), Deianeira sounds an ominous note when she refers to the fear that her beauty might bring disaster upon her (verses 24–25). She would appear to qualify as the good wife, showing constant concern for her husband and giving birth to the children who were the purpose of every Greek marriage (verses 27–31). The latest absence on the part of her husband is the cause for the greatest anxiety. The independence of Heracles and the restrictions which hem in Deianeira are suggested when Hyllus informs his mother of reports that Heracles has been in bondage to a Lydian woman, a double disgrace, for Omphale is a foreigner as well as a woman, and certainly Deianeira responds as if this were the ultimate indignity (verses 69–71). But bondage to a woman may take a variety of forms, one being the chains forged by love, and later in the play it is reported that the destruction of the city of Eurytus was not the consequence of Heracles' subjection to Omphale or the death of Iphitus, but caused by passion for Iole, the daughter of Eurytus (verses 351ff.); Eros, alone of the gods, is said to have been the culprit (verses 354–55). Heracles' passion is subsequently confirmed by Lichas after Deianeira has lulled his fears, stating that she accepts that men are inclined by nature not always to take pleasure in the same things, that Eros is irresistible, and that Heracles has already married other women (verses 436ff.). Iole's beauty has ruined her life as much as Deianeira's own beauty threatened to do so. The song which follows from the chorus tells of the power of love, pressing home the parallel by recounting the story of the clash between Achelous and Heracles (verses 497–530). The plot unfolds with Deianeira attempting to practise magic in order to recover her husband's affection, and the means she employs is the blood of the centaur Nessus, himself another victim of passion, for he was slain by Heracles when he attempted violence against Deianeira (verses 562ff.). The innocent Deianeira brings about her husband's death unwittingly, and so leaves herself no alternative but suicide. Deianeira is certainly no Medea, but passion still wreaks havoc.

A woman left alone is nothing, says the chorus in Aeschylus' *Supplices*; there is no 'Ares' in them (verse 749). Elsewhere in this play the father of these women presents us with the standard Greek view on a woman; after prefacing his remarks with a warning that to speak slander is easy enough, he urges his daughters not to shame him, being of an age which attracts men (verses 995ff.): 'and all, at the sleek comeliness of maidens, do shoot enchanted arrows from their eyes, overcome by desire' (verses 1003–5).5 Men, it seems, are powerless to resist temptations, and women are incapable of not attracting men unless kept under the tightest of control, which in effect means remaining shut up at home. The chorus of the *Choephori* can compile a catalogue of evil women, the daughter of Thestius, the daughter of Nisus, Clytemnestra herself, and the women of Lemnos (verses 602ff.), and the ideal is represented by some words of Orestes, the man is to toil and the wife to stay quietly at home (cf. verse 919). What happens outside the house is man's business, says Eteocles in the *Seven against Thebes*, and a woman must stay within and cause no trouble (verses 200–1; cf. 230–32). The chorus in Sophocles' *Electra* has its own example to add to any list of disreputable women (verses 837ff.), while Tecmessa in the *Ajax* reports words of Ajax which she calls commonplace, silence is a woman's adornment (verses 292–93). No less unambiguous are the words of Macaria in the *Heraclidae* of Euripides: fairest for a woman is silence and modesty, and to remain quietly within the home (verses 476–77). In Sophocles' *Oedipus Coloneus* daughters are forced to assume the burdens normal for sons, as if it were Egypt where men sit at home, and women venture outdoors in search of sustenance (verses 337–41).

Penelope is the prototype of the faithful wife in the *Odyssey*; to contrast with Paris and Helen in the *Iliad*, we have Hector and Andromache. Words put into the mouth of Andromache in Euripides' *Trojan Women* (verses 643–56) not only offer a fuller picture of the ideal, by Greek standards, to which a woman should aspire, but also reveal that that ideal is not as bleak as the previous paragraph may suggest, for its close shows how an element of 'give-and-take' was as much a part of Greek as of modern marriage. This is how Andromache describes her efforts to be a good wife:

But I, who aimed the arrows of ambition high
at honour, and made them good, see now how far I fall,
I, who in Hector's house worked out all custom that brings
discretion's name to women. Blame them or blame them not,

there is one act that swings the scandalous speech their way
beyond all else: to leave the house and walk abroad.
I longed to do it, but put the longing aside, and stayed
always within the inclosure of my own house and court.
The witty speech some women cultivate I would
not practise, but kept my honest inward thought, and made
my mind my only and sufficient teacher. I gave
my lord's presence the tribute of hushed lips, and eyes
quietly downcast. I knew when my will must have its way
over his, knew also how to give way to him in turn.[6]

Such a passage repeats sentiments already encountered in Aeschylus and
Sophocles: the good woman must avoid any possibility of scandalous
talk, must confine herself to the house, must stay silent, and be deferential
in the presence of her husband. I quote it, however, not merely to expand
our understanding of the Greek definition of womanly virtue, and to show
that it differs from our own assessment of woman and her place in society,
thereby emphasizing my argument that it is in terms of Greek values
rather than contemporary values that Greek drama may be appreciated
and its characters and their actions interpreted. I wish, in addition, to
introduce a second question closely related to the discussion of the previous
and also this chapter. To what extent is it meaningful to speak of Euripides
the 'realist'? And here I use the word realist in order to ask how well
Euripides understood human emotions and was able, therefore, to depict
lifelike human beings on the stage. The mention of Euripides and human
emotions immediately suggests a character like Medea or Phaedra, and
it has been his female characters which have earned Euripides the title
'Euripides the psychologist'.[7] Conclusions ought to follow illustration and
argument, but the treatment of the problem of characterization in the
previous chapter will already indicate that Euripides, in my opinion,
hardly qualifies as a realist in any absolute sense, if his claim to any such
description is based on an ability to present in the theatre characters
who expose to the audience the innermost feelings of the human heart.

We marry for love, whatever that may mean, but the Greeks married
to have children and thereby to ensure the continuity of the family. The
different approach demanded by an affair of the heart and by what was
the norm for a Greek, the arranged marriage, is neatly illustrated by the
parasite Chaereas in Menander's *Dyskolos*, when he describes how he
helps a friend in love or wishing to marry: if the friend is in love, and it
has to be in love, with a *hetaera*, a 'courtesan', Chaereas swings into
violent action, carrying her off without argument and without any
questions being asked; if it is marriage, however, which is in prospect,
his response is very different and the parasite makes inquiries after the girl's

family, financial status and disposition, for this is a permanent arrangement (verses 58–68). Marriage, let it be clear, never excluded the possibility of affection and a real union between man and woman. In the sixth book of the *Odyssey*, a poem composed some four hundred years before Menander wrote the *Dyskolos* for the stage, Odysseus gives his own formula for a happy marriage, and, while what he says is conditioned by the fact that he is trying to gain the sympathy of the susceptible Nausicaa, the marriage between Odysseus and Penelope is an example which matches the hero's requirements from marriage, a man and a woman who share house and think in the same way, for Penelope is her husband's equal in guile and in lack of trust (verses 180–85). The arranged marriage is based on a coincidence of social and financial status between the partners in marriage, and the interests they share in common are certain to increase once children are born, giving both a common stake in the future of the family. Society in Western Europe and North America may have abandoned the arranged marriage, but it still persists as a social institution over much of the world, providing a sound foundation for family life. Love is important when the marriage partners are important in their individual right; the arranged marriage is designed to meet the needs of the children of the marriage, and is characteristic of societies where the welfare of the family unit as a whole has precedence over the desires of its senior members.

But what happens in a society where arranged marriages are the rule when a man forms an alliance with a woman of superior status or a woman with a man from a higher social stratum? Such an arrangement threatens trouble, as the chorus in Aeschylus' *Prometheus Vinctus* informs us in the following words: wise is the man who first published this saying, that it is by far the best to ally oneself in marriage in one's own degree; the needy are not to lust after marriage with the pampered wealthy or the proud in lineage (verses 887–93). A marriage between a man who is needy, if only in a relative sense, and a woman of high birth provides Aristophanes with plenty of scope for humour in his *Clouds*, as Strepsiades contrasts his own simple pleasures and aims in life for his son with those of his aristocratic wife (verses 41ff.). Characteristically for the Greek evaluation of woman, the wife is as obsessed with sex as she is with luxuries (see verse 52). The uxorious husband is commonplace in all comic traditions. But one tragedy by Euripides also makes much of a woman married to a husband who is socially far her inferior. I refer to the dramatist's *Electra*. Greek mythology made Electra the wife of Pylades, the closest friend and partner in his return home, of Orestes, and such a marriage is arranged at the end of the drama when the action is tidied up by the gods Castor and Pollux (verse 1249). In the play, however, Electra is shown as married to a farmer. Virginity before the marriage is essential in a Greek bride and so Euripides must have the marriage between Electra and the farmer unconsummated (see verses 43–44 and 255; cf. also verse 1284), an unlikely situation which is explained away by the scruples of a man of ignoble birth allied to a woman of the bluest blood (verses 364–65). And what is already an unlikely situation is not made any more convincing by an outburst from Orestes when he talks of a good father producing a worthless child and evil parents good children, and then proceeds to elaborate on this theme (verses 367ff.).

Electra strikes us, however, as being more of a real person since in the play she comments that when a man comes home from work he likes to find everything inside the house well organized (verses 75–76), our own 'pipe and slippers' attitude, and she also reacts like a modern counterpart, the wife whose husband has come bringing with him, quite unexpectedly, several guests. The household cupboard is inadequately stocked, even bare, and the wife is swift to point out to her husband the deficiencies of her larder. Electra utters the same complaints when her 'husband' wants to entertain guests so impressive as Orestes and Pylades (verses 404–31). Such a detail and so familiar a remark from a wife may make the character of Electra more vivid to the audience, but being more vivid is not the same as being more real. Aeschylus, some fifty years before, can do much the same thing: one of the characters to appear, if only fleetingly, in his *Choephori* is the Nurse (verses 734ff.), and this character has been described by Kitto as 'perhaps the most realistic character in the whole of Greek tragedy'.[8] Elsewhere in commenting on the character of the Nurse, Kitto remarks: 'Aeschylus sketches a character almost Shakespearean in her vividness.'[9] The fact that the word 'sketches' is now deployed suggests a mere outline and no detailed or sustained study in characterization; the Nurse, moreover, has now become vivid rather than real. Lloyd-Jones, who is no believer in the individualism of Aeschylean characterization and rejects the view that the pursuit of psychological depth was the poet's purpose, is content to note the Nurse's 'vivacious garrulity and a readiness to mention humble objects and pursuits'.[10] The Nurse, it should be added, is not an exceptional example in the surviving plays by the earliest of the three great tragedians from fifth-century Athens: in the *Agamemnon*, for instance, the Herald is just as prosaic in recounting the hardships experienced by the troops encamped before Troy (verses 555ff.). In short, touches which seem to be realistic because they refer to the common things of life, and things common among us as they were common among the Greeks, and touches which transport us from a heroic to an everyday world are present in Greek drama as early as Aeschylus and certainly are not peculiar to Euripides.

Everything is too sudden and too extreme in Euripides to be realistic in
an absolute sense; we are moving in an atmosphere where the triumphant
Aegisthus not only rides in Agamemnon's chariot and holds his sceptre,
but also, in his drunkenness, is reported to jump on his predecessor's
grave, to throw stones at the monument, and to pour abuse on the head of
the absent Orestes (*Electra*, 319ff.).

The words put in the mouth of Euripides in Aristophanes' *Frogs*
suggests that perhaps he earned the reputation of being realistic because
his characters perform normal, everyday activities, including talking to
excess (cf. verses 959ff.)! Electra's reaction at the sight of unexpected
and imposing guests is just such an activity, and it is dangerous on the
grounds of evidence so flimsy to start discussing the plays of Euripides
as if he were a fifth-century precursor of Chekhov. He has no greater
claim to be thought an ancient version of Henrik Ibsen. Creusa in the
Ion may tug at our hearts as we see repeated in her anguished story the
plight of a woman of today who has an illegitimate child, is abandoned
by the father, is forced to have her child adopted, and then, twenty or
more years later, remains obsessed by a desire to establish contact with
the long-lost son once again; Ion himself in the same play, I do not deny,
is capable of moving us deeply as we recall, perhaps from a personal
knowledge, the yearning of an adopted child to identify his true parent,
the actual mother to whom he owes his own birth. But the character of
neither Creusa nor Ion is sketched in more than broad outline; we know
about both of them only as much as we need to know if their story is to
have the maximum impact as dramatic entertainment. Again, we must
not be deceived into reading too much between the lines if in a tragedy
such as the *Hippolytus* Euripides appears to explain the attitude of his
characters in terms both of hereditary traits and environment. In the
course of this play we are reminded of the strain of passion which afflicted
both Phaedra's mother, Pasiphae, and her sister, Ariadne (verses 337–43),
and to which Phaedra herself is now to succumb, its third victim; we
also see how Phaedra is an aristocratic lady with time on her hands
during which to brood and to become obsessive (verses 373ff.). And
Hippolytus is the son of an Amazon, a bastard child, and brought up
not by his father Theseus but by a foster parent (verses 10–11, 307–9,
351, 581, 962–63 and 1455). But, in the case of both Phaedra and Hippolytus, these are broad strokes of the poet's brush, and his technique is
impressionistic rather than representational.

But if we return to the *Electra*, one further passage and one further
point of detail in that play will provide us with an even clearer idea of
the type of realism which is to be associated with Euripides. Half-way
through the play Orestes is recognized as her brother by Electra (verses

508ff.). In Aeschylus' *Choephori* the corresponding scene has as its recognition tokens a lock of hair, foot-print and clothes (verses 168ff., 205ff. and 231ff.). In the *Electra* these tokens are advanced in turn by the Old Man to prove to Electra that Orestes has come home, and each in turn is rejected by Electra as absurd (verses 515ff., 532ff. and 539ff.): the lock of hair because the hair of young men and women are not the same, and many who are not related have similar hair; the foot-print because stony ground does not yield foot-prints and a man's foot, anyway, is larger than a woman's; the possibility of Orestes wearing clothes woven by Electra because Electra was young when Orestes was banished, and Orestes who had grown up in exile could hardly still be wearing clothes which had fitted him so many years ago. All this is pre-eminently logical: indeed it is worthy of the scholar who sits in his study poring over a text but never actually going to a theatre, for it is as finicky as it is logical. Euripides prefers a personal recognition by the Old Man, which is confirmed, and here the dramatist follows a good Homeric precedent, by the token offered by a scar (verses 558ff.). The scar is an effective proof and has, further, a symbolic value, since Orestes suffered it from a fall when 'pursuing a fawn in his father's house' (verses 573–74), and he and Electra are soon to join in the hunt for their father's murderers (cf. verses 581–82). In Aristotelian terms this recognition falls into the first class of *anagnorisis* (*Poetics* 1454b 19ff.) and, as the philosopher goes on to add, this is the type of recognition most frequently used because of poverty of invention, that is, recognition by visible signs, though, in defence of Euripides, it must be marked that Aristotle refers to the Homeric and not this Euripidean scar. The *Choephori* example, however, is recognition 'on the basis of reasoning' (*Poetics* 1455a 4ff.), and such a recognition is ranked second only to the recognition arising from the actions alone. My own criticism of the recognition of Orestes, as handled by Euripides, is that its closing stage is excessively hurried. The previous scepticism of Electra, although it appears to be deep-rooted, crumbles away with a surprising rapidity, leading to an acceptance which is too abrupt to carry conviction. The fact that brother and sister meet and talk together much earlier in the play (verses 220ff.) and that Electra at one point in such a long exchange claims that she would not recognize him if she were to see Orestes (verse 283) makes her eventual acknowledgement of her brother that much more sudden.[11] The dramatic cry 'I am convinced by your tokens' (verses 577–78) enables Euripides to hurry on with his story with an almost indecent haste, and such would seem to be the dramatist's actual intention. The potential inherent in a situation has been exhausted, and Electra changes her opinion with a rapidity which we have already seen elsewhere (see our pp. 61–62). Euripides may criticize

Aeschylus for a lack of realism in the recognition scene from the *Choephori*, but Euripides' handling of the same motif is itself more than a little suspect if drama may be legitimately criticized on such grounds. Euripidean realism is something of a mirage which quickly disappears as we look more searchingly at it.

And then there is the matter of Electra's pot. In both his earliest comedy to have survived, the *Acharnians*, and again in the latest fifth-century comedy by Aristophanes, the *Frogs*, this comic dramatist ridicules Euripides' penchant for dressing his characters in beggar's rags (e.g. *Acharnians*, 412ff.). In the *Electra* the heroine of that play appears on stage dressed in rags (verse 185); even more devastatingly, Electra enters carrying on her head a pot (verse 55) like any serving woman (cf. verses 107–9). Like the wreath worn by the man who returns from an oracle bearing good news (see our p. 46), these are unsophisticated props, and neither rags nor pot in themselves can add much in the way of realism to a stage and a setting as neutral and as colourless as those we associate with the Greek theatre, though they may contribute to an illusion of reality. To equip Electra with a domestic utensil of a kind which Greek peasant women can still be seen carrying on their heads today as they make their way to the village well, and thereby to suggest that she has been reduced to the level of a farmer's wife is not to make her character more realistic but to make the background and circumstances of the story unheroic, and this is what Euripidean realism so often amounts to, an unheroic presentation of character or plot. Electra works as any farmer's wife works, but not because she has to, but in order to proclaim to the world the indignities heaped upon her (verses 57–59; cf. 302ff.). Her husband, scrupulous as he is, does not want her to toil away, and, when she insists, consoles himself (or is he humouring Electra?) with an observation that the spring is no distance from the house (77–78). This is scarcely an 'heroic' comment.

Rags and the pot, of course, do serve a dramatic purpose, contrasting with the appearance of Clytemnestra, another woman who has married beneath herself in replacing Agamemnon with Aegisthus, when she first arrives on stage in the *Electra* (verse 966; cf. also verse 1107, and further verses 304ff.), and it is dramatic effect, not the hope that characters will be more realistic, which is important. The lack of food with which to entertain unexpected guests also serves a dramatic function: it leads Electra to instruct her husband to search out the Old Man who is going eventually to recognize Orestes (verses 409ff.). So too does the failure on the part of Electra and the farmer to consummate their marriage; as well as preserving Electra's virginity for Pylades, it enables the playwright to exploit dramatic irony, for Clytemnestra is persuaded to visit her

daughter and therefore dies (verses 651ff.), because she believes Electra
to have given birth to a son, and, it will be remembered, this marriage
between unequals was intended to prevent Electra from having children
likely to avenge their grandfather (verses 19ff.). Euripides is fond of
dressing his characters in a particular costume in order to achieve a
special effect and not for the sake of realism. Thus in the *Andromache*
Hermione wears a golden crown and an embroidered robe, part of the
dowry given by her father Menelaus to guarantee her freedom of speech,
whereas Andromache is slave and captive (verses 147ff.); in the *Helen*
the shipwrecked Menelaus seems to be dressed in bits of ship-sail (verse
422), and this proves useful later when he has to report his own fake death
(verses 1079–81; cf. also Helen's change of costume, verses 1088 and 1186–
87); especially exotic and, I would think, totally unrealistic is the ingenious
disguise of a wolf's skin adopted by Dolon in the *Rhesus* in order to carry
out his excursion into enemy territory (verses 208ff.). Incongruous, and
therefore dramatic, is the appearance of the old men, Teiresias and Cad-
mus, when in the *Bacchae* they assume the Bacchic costume of thrysus,
fawn-skin and ivy crown (verses 176–77, 180, 205 and 249–54), and even
more obviously dramatic is Pentheus himself attired as one of Dionysus'
female worshippers (verses 827ff. and 912ff.).

Euripides could have made an adequate contrast between the splendidly
dressed Clytemnestra and her filthy and ragged daughter without any
need to introduce the pot on Electra's head, and this piece of equipment
does seem dangerously like what we currently call a 'gimmick', and a gimmick is nothing more than a dramatist's trick. Certainly in other Greek
plays we can see stage props whose function is more clearly dramatic.
One thinks of the sword with which Sophocles' Ajax commits suicide
in the tragedy of that name (see verses 658ff., 815ff. and 1024ff.),[12]
or the urn which holds the spurious ashes of Orestes in the same playwright's *Electra* (see verses 54–58 and 757ff.). In Euripides we have letters
in the Hippolytus and the two *Iphigenia* plays (verses 856ff.; *I.A.*, 34ff.;
I.T., 727ff.), the wine-skin in the *Cyclops* (verses 145ff.), and in the *Bacchae*
the severed head of Pentheus (verses 1168ff.). The first and last of these
props, the sword of Ajax and the head of Pentheus, have a special significance, one because it is the actual instrument of death and the other
because it is so gruesome, but all the others as well surpass Electra's pot
in dramatic force.

We have not exhausted the information which the *Electra* has to offer
about the position of women in Greek society. We might also have referred to lines 343–44, when the farmer seeing strangers in conversation
with his wife comments that it is disgraceful for a woman to stand with
young men, or to lines 932–33 in which Electra states that it is disgraceful

for a woman and not the man to be in charge of the house, or to lines
1036–40 in which Clytemnestra points out that a double and different
standard is applied when men and women seek love outside the home,
or to lines 1052–53 whose speaker is the chorus and in which it is said
that the woman who is sensible ought to agree with her husband in every
respect. Other plays by Euripides which have survived, and here I exclude
the *Medea* and the *Hippolytus*, since the characters after whom both plays
are named argue from a particular, prejudiced point of view, confirm that
the picture of a woman's position in society offered by the *Electra* is
a fair one and a typical one. That a woman should not be seen abroad is
illustrated by the beginning of the *Phoenissae* when the *paidagogos* is
anxious to check whether there is anybody about to see Antigone, who
has come out of her quarters within the palace to survey the attacking
forces (verses 88ff.), while in the *Orestes* it is remarked that it is 'not
proper that maidens should venture among a throng' (verses 108). Female
modesty can be carried to such a pitch that it strikes a modern reader as
being simply absurd: thus in the *Hecuba* a messenger, describing the
death of Polyxena, having already detailed how this woman tore open
her dress to expose her breasts, proceeds to observe that Polyxena at
the moment of death had the great forethought to fall to the ground
gracefully, 'concealing what ought to be concealed from the eyes of men'
(verses 568–70). Iphigenia acknowledges the inferiority of her sex in the
Iphigenia in Aulis (verse 1394), while in the *Supplices* we read that the
wise woman does everything at man's direction (verses 40–41). At the
same time a woman's ability to cause trouble for men is acknowledged
in the *Orestes*, the speaker being a chorus of women (verses 605–6),
and in the other *Iphigenia* play women are described as being terrible
at devising tricks (verses 1032). Some idea of the 'weapons' on which
they lay their hands, the sword, deceit, poison, is conveyed by the words
of the Old Man in the *Ion* (verses 843–46). Of course, as we learn from
the same tragedy, there are good women and bad women, but all are
hated (verse 398–400). An obvious example of the good women is provided
by Andromache, and earlier (see our pp. 83–84) I quoted words spoken
by this wife in the *Trojan Women*, actually verses 643–56, in order to
show how the ideal demanded that a woman keep her reputation intact
by not venturing outside the home and thereby exposing herself to risk,
and that a woman remain silent and subdued in the presence of her husband, while, as is shown clearly by the concluding words of the extract, in
practice complete independence of mind and opinion was not sacrificed,
for Andromache speaks of knowing when she had to prevail over
Hector as well as when she had to give way to her male partner (verses
655–56). She carried on by saying that her qualities as a wife have led to

the son of Achilles, her husband's killer, wanting her with the result
that she will become a slave in the house of the murderers (verses 657ff.).
Andromache's dilemma is impossible; either she is to betray her love
for Hector or she is to be hated by her masters. 'And yet', she adds,
'they say that one night slackens a woman's hatred of a man's bed'
(verses 665–66). Women, in the opinion of the Greek, are over-sexed,
and their obsession with Eros, with Aphrodite, is equally disastrous to
both sexes, especially if on the one hand we have a woman and on the
other a young man (cf. *Hippolytus*, 967–69).

If I have spent some time discussing the Greek attitude towards women,
as it is revealed in drama, it is because this is probably the most effective
way to show that we must interpret Greek plays and we must discuss
'characterization' in them in terms of Greek values and not our own
values. The wife is an essential element in the family group, and I might
have preferred to follow others in considering the family and the part it
plays in the dramatic tradition of fifth-century Athens.[13] If I had, my
discussion would have begun with Aristotle, who in the *Poetics*, having
posed the question 'What arouses fear or pity?', tells us that what we should
look for is a situation involving those closely connected, a brother killing
a brother, a son killing a father, a mother killing a son, or a son killing
a mother (1453b 19–22). But I wish to leave this on one side so that one
more aspect of Euripides' 'realism' may be briefly investigated, and here
again I shall begin with a comment made by Aristotle. In the *Poetics* the
dramatist's treatment of the chorus is considered, and, though what the
philosopher has to say is slight, it is relevant to the question of Euripidean
realism: 'One should regard the chorus too as one of the actors, and as
part of the whole and taking part in the action; that is, one should follow
Sophocles' practice rather than Euripides' ' (1456a 25–27). It is likely
that critics have this passage very much in the forefront of their minds
when, for all his supposed realism, they criticize Euripides for a failure
to integrate his chorus with the main action of his plot.[14] Secrets are
revealed in the hearing of a chorus of women, hardly the safest and, therefore, the most convincing guarantee that a secret will be kept: in the *Ion*, for
example, the chorus does betray a secret (cf. verses 666–67 and 757–807),
while in the *Electra* Orestes has to ask whether the chorus is to be trusted
and to receive the assurance of his sister (verses 272–73). With our mention
of the chorus we have touched upon the kernel of Greek drama, the
nucleus from which it evolved as actor, and later actors, joined chorus.
A chorus can never be a realistic component of theatrical entertainment.
The Greeks in the fifth century B.C. did not question the presence in
the orchestra of the chorus. How many audiences in a modern theatre
can tolerate it? In the first chapter I said that the modern play which

most closely resembles a Greek tragedy in its structure is Eliot's *Murder in the Cathedral* (see our p. 5), and in that play, of course, we have a chorus. Eliot admits two reasons for depending heavily upon the assistance offered by the chorus in *Murder in the Cathedral*. One is the fact that a poet who becomes for the first time a dramatist feels happier with choral verse than with dramatic dialogue. The first reason which he advances is, however, more interesting and certainly very instructive for Greek drama and its use of a chorus. 'The first was that the essential action of the play—both the historical facts and the matter which I invented—was somewhat limited. A man comes home, foreseeing that he will be killed, and he is killed. I did not want to increase the number of characters, I did not want to write a chronicle of twelfth-century politics, nor did I want to tamper unscrupulously with the meagre records . . . I wanted to concentrate on death and martyrdom. The introduction of a chorus of excited and sometimes hysterical women, reflecting in their emotion the significance of the action, helped wonderfully.'[15] Is Eliot's use of his chorus so very different from that of his Greek counterpart? A chorus introduces another dimension into a play and one which contrasts strongly with the scenes separating the songs of the chorus: 'logical' debate between a pair of characters on stage is thrown into sharper relief when what divides scene from scene is a collective song couched in a wealth of metaphorical language and imagery. The plots of Greek tragedy are simple and action concentrated and, as a result, scope for characterization is limited. We concentrate on the essentials, and the chorus helps us to concentrate on these essentials.

NOTES

1 *Shakespeare without Words and Other Essays* (Cambridge, Mass., 1972), p. 3. I discuss Greek values, concentrating, however, on Homer and Hesiod and the evidence to be found in their poetry, in *Greek Peasants, Ancient and Modern* (Manchester, 1970). See also K. J. Dover, *Greek Popular Morality in the Time of Plato and Aristotle* (Oxford, 1974). The principles and methods to be employed when social evidence is extracted from literature are considered by Joan Rockwell, *Fact in Fiction, the use of literature in the systematic study of society* (London, 1974).

2 A. W. H. Adkins, *Classical Quarterly* 16 (1966), p. 208.

3 I quote the translation by David Grene in the Chicago series, *Euripides* (1955), p. 182.

4 Juliet du Boulay, *Portrait of a Greek Mountain Village* (Oxford, 1974), p. 81.

5 As translated by S. G. Benardete, *Aeschylus II* (Chicago, 1956), p. 40.

6 The translation quoted is that by Richmond Lattimore in the Chicago series, *Euripides III* (1958), p. 151.

7 See, for example, Werner Jaeger, *Paideia, the Ideals of Greek Culture I* (Oxford, 1939), pp. 341ff., who at one point dubs Euripides the first psychologist (p. 350).

8 This comment appears in the first edition of *Greek Tragedy* (London, 1939), p. 83, in a chapter on the *Oresteia* rewritten for the third edition (1961), where the Nurse has been reduced to 'a lifelike character', p. 85.

9 *Form and Meaning in Drama* (London,[2] 1964), p. 51; cf. *Greek Tragedy* (1961), with its reference to 'this vivid sketch', p. 85.

10 In his Prentice-Hall edition of the *Libation Bearers* (1970), p. 7; cf. ibid. pp. 5–7, and the companion edition of the *Agamemnon* (1970), pp. 6–8.

11 The recognition scenes in the *Choephori* and the two *Electras* have recently been compared by F. Solmsen, *Electra and Orestes, Three Recognitions in Greek Tragedy* (Amsterdam, 1967), who argues (pp. 9ff.) that the recognition of Orestes by Electra in Euripides' play is delayed again and again, and that our expectations are constantly disappointed. His argument strengthens my own statement that the recognition, when it finally comes, is surprisingly speedy.

12 On Ajax and his sword, see Lattimore, *The Poetry of Greek Tragedy* (Baltimore, 1958), pp. 75–77.

13 John Jones, *On Aristotle and Greek Tragedy*, is especially suggestive in considering this subject.

14 Typical are the comments of Gilbert Murray, *Euripides and his Age* (London), pp. 228ff.

15 *On Poetry and Poets* (London, 1957), pp. 80–81.

Drama and the Athenian Background

EARLY in this study I attempted an answer to the question of how long it took to stage a play at the City Dionysia in the fifth century B.C. This question is not as interesting as the various other questions which have arisen in the course of our discussion. What is to be understood as 'reality' in terms of the Greek theatre is a problem which has increasingly absorbed our attention as we have sought to place the dramatic tradition of the Greeks in both its theatrical and its social context. In chapter one it was argued that a Greek play did reproduce real life in the eyes of the spectators. Again, consideration of the spoken word and its predominant position as a vehicle of communication called into question the opinion that the Greeks banished from their stage acts of violence because they were incapable of staging such incidents convincingly, that is, in a realistic manner. An investigation of acting and actors further advanced our understanding of realism in the ancient theatre, while comments on social values and the status of women in Greek society led to an assessment of Euripides' claim to the title 'Euripides the realist'.

At the same time we have also noted the frequent echoes of contemporary life, of activities characteristic of the assembly and law-courts, in particular plays. The Greek tragedians were indifferent to what we would class as anachronisms, allowing them by the score to 'disfigure' their writings. Shakespeare, of course, is no less guilty. A good example of such an anachronism is offered by the opening words spoken by Agamemnon in Aeschylus' play of the same name (verses 810ff.). This monarch refers to the gods having placed their votes in the 'urn of blood', thereby sealing the fate of the city of Troy (verses 813–16; cf. *Eumenides*, 741–43). In the passage the gods are imagined as functioning as a juryman functioned in the court of law at Athens, dropping his pebble in one of two containers to signify either condemnation or acquittal. Slightly later Agamemnon talks of calling general meetings and deliberating in full assembly (verses 844–46), posing as a king whose powers are constitutionally restricted, very much as Pelagus, king of Argos, does in Aeschylus' *Supplices* (e.g. verses 365–69). This sounds equally anachronistic. But our first example is better than the second, since Agamemnon seems to represent a Homeric-type king rather than what we mean by a constitutional monarch. More important than a particular case, I would argue, is the general question whether or not we are justified in applying the description anachronism whenever we come across a practice to be associated with the fifth century in a play whose setting is the heroic past. Let me explain the reason for my disquiet, though it will probably be apparent if the reader remembers how vague the Greeks were in distinguishing between different times of the day (see our p. 13): precise chronology preoccupied the ancients much less than it does us. In addition, Greek mythology is mythology pure and simple to us; to the Greeks it represented history. Agamemnon, Clytemnestra, Orestes and the rest were thought to have actually lived, ruling over Mycenae and the other states of the heroic age. A knowledge of these persons and events, moreover, was not preserved by means of written documents but by oral transmission, being handed down by word of mouth as generation succeeded generation and as stories were told and retold. It is inevitable that orally preserved knowledge should be constantly updated: what was unimportant, uninteresting or unintelligible was discarded in favour of what did interest the listener and could be understood by the listener in the light of his own experience of life. If there was a united attack by the Greeks against Troy, the Greeks followed Agamemnon because Mycenaean society was feudal in structure and military service was demanded of lesser lords. Greek society lost its feudal character after the Mycenaean period, and so a new explanation had to be found to account for the willingness of the Greeks to follow Agamemnon across the Aegean Sea. This new explanation portrayed the princes of Greece (with the exception of Achilles) as the suitors of Helen and bound by an oath to uphold the rights of whomever her father Tyndareus was persuaded to select from the competing suitors as the husband of Helen. It is the Homeric poems, beyond all else, which illustrate the process of updating orally transmitted traditions: a few Mycenaean reminiscences can be identified if we examine the material and social milieu of the *Iliad* and the *Odyssey*, but much more frequent are references to artifacts and customs dating several centuries after the supposed period of time when Troy was besieged and destroyed. Many would see a great deal of Homer's own eighth century in the contents of the poems.

Drama is a living force and not static. The Greek dramatist, like his Elizabethan counterpart, may take his plot from the past, but he interpreted events with one eye firmly fixed on the political and social climate of his own lifetime. Shakespeare, for instance, reflects in his historical plays the belief of the contemporary Englishman in the divine right of kings, while Aeschylus in the *Eumenides* can exploit the recently concluded alliance between Athens and Argos (see verses 289ff., 669ff. and 762ff.) and the change in powers of the Areopagus. The playwrights of both ages were not restricted by any need to maintain the standards of fidelity and accuracy required from those who write history. By blending imperceptibly together past and present they achieved a semblance of reality which is the more effective because it is not factually real. And so in the *Poetics* Aristotle writes (1451a 38–b 11): 'The difference between the historian and the poet is not merely that one writes verse and the other prose— one could turn Herodotus' work into verse and it would be just as much history as before; the essential difference is that the one tells us what happened and the other the sort of thing that would happen. That is why poetry is at once more like philosophy and more worth while than history, since poetry tends to make general statements, while those of history are particular. A "general statement" means one that tells us what sort of man would, probably or necessarily, say or do what sort of thing, and this is what poetry aims at, though it attaches proper names; a particular statement on the other hand tells us what Alcibiades, for instance, did or what happened to him.' In an earlier chapter (see our pp. 54–56) we spoke of the typical characters, particularly the stock tragedy-tyrant, to be seen everywhere in Greek drama, and this quotation from Aristotle reveals what is to be gained from not individualizing to excess the personages who appear on stage as a play unfolds.

The contemporary references in the *Eumenides* are marked by a strong streak of jingoism. Aeschylus, we are often told, shared in the confidence of mid-fifth-century Athens, an Athens which had witnessed the Persian enemy expelled from mainland Greece and the region of the Aegean Sea, and an Athens securely set on the threshold of imperial grandeur, and so we have surviving a play such as this poet's *Persae* (see, for example, the jingoism manifested by verses 230–45). But Sophocles and Euripides, even at the very end of the same century, when disaster faced Athens on every side, may give voice to sentiments no less jingoistic in tone. 'In so far as a political situation was made the subject of Tragedy at all, propriety demanded that it should be treated with optimism and confidence.'[1] The most obvious exception to the rule that tragedy-tyrants lack self-control, are horribly suspicious, and rely too often on brute force is provided by the presentation in Greek drama of king Theseus of Athens. Just as the recovery of the bones of Orestes in the sixth century set the seal on growing Spartan imperialism, so the discovery in the seventies of the fifth century of the bones of the hero Theseus, who had already, or so tradition records, put in a fleeting appearance on the battle-field of Marathon, announced the arrival of an expansionist Athens.[2] Theseus is featured as the national hero and as a focus for loyalty on the part of the citizens of the Athenian state, an enlightened and constitutional monarch, in Sophocles' *Oedipus Coloneus* and Euripides' *Supplices*. In these two plays his qualities are more clearly displayed because of the contrast drawn between Theseus and the despotic, cringing, hypocritical Creon of Thebes.

The *Oedipus Coloneus* dates from the very end of the fifth century B.C., having been produced after Sophocles' death in 406. Early in the play the blind Oedipus asks a question which would be nonsensical if this were in any way a realistic play, and a question, furthermore, the second half of which surely counts as an anachronism: 'Who is the ruler here or is authority vested in the people?' (verse 66). The answer he receives is Theseus, son of Aegeus. Theseus is presented on stage as the physical embodiment not only of the power of Athens but also of its statescraft, for he is more than a St. George figure, who rescues the daughters of Oedipus. He is the astutest of politicians as well, since, by providing a resting place for the body of Oedipus, Athens stands to gain, as Oedipus himself states on more than one occasion (verses 72, 287–88 and 579ff.). Oedipus need have no fear that Theseus will not come and see him (cf. verses 299ff.), for Theseus is quick to sieze any opportunity. Like any other Greek, Theseus treasures success (see our pp. 77ff.), and, while his own career may make him sympathetic towards a suppliant (verses 562–68), he can strike a note which hardly suggests nobility of character in our eyes. Thus, when Theseus re-appears as Antigone is threatened with abduction, he orders forces to be summoned in case he becomes a laughing stock, having been overcome by force (verses 902–3), although he attaches to this remark a flattering comment on Athens, a city which practices justice and ordains nothing without the support of law (verses 913–14). Fear of ridicule, however typical of the Greeks such a sentiment may be, is not much of a moral incentive to action, and is an emotion shared in this same play by Oedipus' disreputable son, the ill-fated Polyneices (verses 1422–23). Yet this is a Greek play, and only Greek values are relevant.

The hypothesis which precedes our text of Euripides' *Supplices* calls this drama an encomium of the Athenians. Certainly Theseus eulogizes contemporary Athens no less fervidly than Pericles does in his Funeral Speech when in the *Supplices* he claims that no *tyrannos* rules at Athens and that the city is free, not being under the control of a single man (verses 403ff.). When he goes on to add that the people rule in turn by annual succession and that the claims of wealth are ignored, the poor man having equal power, the context of these remarks is blatantly that of the contemporary Athenian democracy. In the play Theseus respects the common laws of Greece, the right of the chieftains killed in Polyneices' attack on Thebes to burial, although their bodies were secured for internment only after a battle with the army of Creon. Theseus is persuaded to do this by the entreaties of his mother Aethra, who added her pleas to those already uttered by Adrastus, king of Argos and father-in-law of Polyneices. Every Greek drama is a product of its own times, even of the very year in which it was first presented on the stage. The *Supplices* of Euripides is

virulently anti-Theban, and it is difficult not to associate its story of the
Thebans refusing burial to fallen enemies with this state's refusal to
surrender the bodies of the Athenian dead after the battle of Delium in
424 B.C.[3] Any play which depicts the Thebans committing a comparable
outrage would have had an immediate impact, if it were staged at one of
the drama festivals of the next few years.

The story told in the *Supplices* and Theseus' determination to uphold
the common laws of humanity even though it leads to war certainly
suggests that the Athenian cuts an heroic figure in the play, and so, in my
opinion, he does. Yet one critic has argued 'that the portrait of Theseus
is not quite what it has usually been taken to be'.[4] The case made in support
of such an eccentric opinion is interesting because it betrays an ignorace of
much of what I have been attempting to illustrate throughout. Thus it is
claimed that Theseus 'is very ready to *lecture* (my own italics) the un-
happy Adrastus', [5] and it is suggested that we may be inclined to sympathize with the 'gentle but dignified protest' which Adrastus voices in
verses 253–56. Of course, Theseus does lecture the king of Argos in the
long speech which runs from verse 195 to verse 249, but then characters
in Greek plays regularly 'lecture', rather than converse with, another
person on the stage (see our pp. 27ff.), and Theseus' words provide a
splendid rhetorical set-piece, being full of the kind of sentiments a contemporary audience would warmly welcome. The passage opens with a
sketch from Theseus of the beginnings of civilized life which develops into
an attack on Adrastus because he was foolish enough to marry his daugthers
to strangers, mixing what was pure with what was impure (verses
201–28). When Theseus says that the wise man ought to look to the
prosperous when it comes to marriage, he is simply affirming a basic
principle of the arranged marriage. What he then proceeds to add about the
folly of launching the expedition against Thebes (verses 229ff.) is common
sense, and it also allows him to comment on the three types of citizens
(verses 238ff.), the rich and useless, the poor and envious, and the class
which preserves cities, those in the middle. This is conventional Greek
'wisdom' of the 'nothing to excess' kind, well calculated to appeal to the
prejudices of a popular audience, and not unlike the description of the
various speakers at the trial of Orestes, as reported in the play of that
name similarly by Euripides (see our p. 38).

Greenwood is also bothered because Theseus has his share of vanity
and treats Creon's herald abusively, believing 'that Theseus is *deliberately*
set *well* (my own italics) below the level of the heroic, and even, here and
there, made a little ridiculous'.[6] It is true that Theseus 'blows his own
trumpet' and blows it hard (e.g. verses 337ff.), but there is nothing exceptional in this: it is characteristic of a society in which personal prestige is

of a crucial importance that its members should seek to promote their reputations. Honour depends upon its being recognized by others, and one's reputation must be spread abroad, and each individual will share in the process of spreading his own fame. Violence, as was said in the previous chapter (see our pp. 79ff.), was accepted by the Greeks as perfectly normal human behaviour, and this should be borne in mind when we consider Theseus' attitude towards his opponent, the herald sent by Thebes. The dispute between Theseus and the herald is very much a set debate, a contest of arguments (see verses 427–28), in which the relative merits of single-man government and democracy are compared. Here we meet a picture of fifth-century Athens which is anachronistic to the point of including an allusion to the formula used when people were invited to speak before the assembly (verses 438–39). If the herald is insulted and threatened (see verses 426, 458–62 and 566–67), surely he gets what, in the opinion of the original audience, he deserved. If his argument carries some degree of conviction, it serves the dramatic purpose of making this altercation absolutely absorbing. Against this we must set Theseus' role in the battle subsequently fought (verses 707ff.), his humility in burying those killed in that battle (verses 759ff.), and the consideration which he shows to the mothers of the Seven once their bodies have been recovered (verses 942–46).

We also noted in chapter six that one insult leads to a second insult in retaliation (see our pp. 78ff.), and the same principle of reciprocity applies to favours: the man of honour who receives a favour is admitting his inferiority and is obliged to re-assert his prestige by responding with an equivalent or a more generous favour. An example of this concept of mutual obligations and the exchange of favours is offered by Theseus when he speaks the following words to the chorus and his mother Aethra (verses 361–64):

> A wretched child
> is he who does not return his parents' care.
> Noblest of gifts! By granting it, he earns
> back from his children what he gives his parents.[7]

Such obligations exist not only between individuals but also between states. When Theseus hands over the remains of the Seven he stresses this very point (verses 1169–75):

> You, who behold what you have gained from me,
> must keep this act in grateful recollection,
> and tell your children constantly to honour
> this city, handing down from son to son
> the memory of answered prayers. Zeus
> and the gods in heaven know the kindnesses
> of which we thought you worthy. Go in peace.

And Adrastus, in reply, accepts this obligation (verses 1176–79), saying that the Argives admit an undying gratitude for

> We have been nobly treated
> by you, and owe you action in return.

As if on cue, the goddess Athene appears and instructs Theseus not to return the bones before he has received an oath that the Argives will never attack Athens and that, if others attack Athens, they will oppose the assailants (verses 1185ff.). This is not, as Greenwood claims, an instruction which degrades Theseus' recovery of the bodies 'into a sordid bargain for the solid advantage of Athens', although he is correct in calling the part of Athene purely an epilogue.[8] Yet another level of reality is to be seen when the gods and goddesses of the Greeks, with the notable exception of Zeus, parade in the Theatre of Dionysus. But at the conclusion of the *Supplices* the appearance of Athene, the patron deity of Athens, is no instance of a *deus ex machina* being introduced by a dramatist otherwise unable to sort out a hopelessly contorted situation. This 'contrivance' should be employed, according to Aristotle (*Poetics* 1454b 2–6), 'for things outside the play, either all that happened beforehand that a human being could not know, or all that happens later and needs foretelling and reporting; for we attribute omniscience to the gods', and this is how it is employed in the *Supplices*, since Athene goes on to predict the successful assault on Thebes by the Epigoni (verses 1213–26). It also, of course, gives us Athene, the parton saint, as well as Theseus, the national hero, in the play, and, further, furnishes the drama with a resounding conclusion. It is not unlike, for example, the epiphany of Athene in the *Ion*, in which Ion and Cresa have already identified each other. Ion may have lingering doubts as to his father's identity, but the goddess' intervention is primarily a device whereby a patriotic poet may acclaim the Athenian ancestry of various divisions of the Greek people (verses 1575ff.). This is another passage strongly marked by jingoistic sentiments to add to Ion's earlier reference to the freedom of speech characteristic of the Athenian state (verses 670–75).

Theseus is returning a favour himself when he appears in support of Heracles in the *Hercules Furens* (verses 1169–71, 1220–25 and 1336–37). Such a man ought one to obtain as a friend, says Heracles, a comment converted into general praise of Athens by Amphitryon, when he says in the following line, 'a land which bore such a man is a land of fair progeny' (verses 1404–5). The *Heraclidae* is concerned with the next generation, the children of Heracles and Theseus' son Demophon, who acts as their protector, so perpetuating the nobility of his family (cf. verses 320–28). Aegeus, the father of Theseus, appears in the *Medea*, when he is persuaded to offer that woman a place of refuge at Athens (verses 663ff.). This encounter is obviously meant to contrast with the earlier scene in which Medea, again exercising her considerable powers of persuasion, wrings the concession of a further day's stay in Corinth from Creon, king of that city (verses 271ff.). Creon is a fool; he is making a mistake and knows that he is making a mistake (verses 350–51). Aegeus, on the other hand, stands to gain from his generosity, for Medea undertakes to give him children (verses 717–18 and 721), and even then Aegeus will have nothing to do with Medea's escape from Corinth itself, since he, astute politician that he, like his son Theseus, is, has no wish to incur blame (verse 730). The oath that they go on to exchange is mutually advantageous: it offers the one a guaranteed retreat and the other a convenient excuse (verses 731–45). The *Medea* was produced in 431 B.C., the year in which war broke out between Athens and Sparta, and it is not insignificant that the scene between Medea and Aegeus is followed by the justly most celebrated ode in praise of Athens, its people, climate and culture (verses 824–45):

> From of old the children of Erechtheus are
> splendid, the sons of blessed gods. They dwell
> in Athens' holy and unconquered land,
> where famous Wisdom feeds them and they pass gaily
> always through that most brilliant air where once, they say,
> that golden Harmony gave birth to the nine
> pure Muses of Pieria.
>
> And beside the sweet flow of Cephisus' stream,
> where Cyprus sailed, they say, to draw the water
> and mild soft breezes breathed along her path,
> and on her hair were flung the sweet-smelling garlands
> of flowers of roses by the Lovers, the companions
> of Wisdom, her escort, the helpers of men
> in every kind of excellence.[9]

But praise of Athens is only one side of the picture; there is also attack on the enemies of the Athenian state, and we have already seen both Thebans and Corinthians denounced in the person of their kings. It was the Spartans, however, who are to be thought Athens' main opponents. In the *Supplices* Adrastus explains why an appeal for help has been addressed to Athens: Sparta, it seems, is cruel and her ways artful, while other states are small and weak (verses 187–88). Much fiercer is the denunciation of the Spartans in the *Andromache*, a play which appears to have been produced just a couple of years before the *Supplices*. There Andromache can call these Greeks crafty, liars, plotters, perverse, murderers, grasping and devious (verses 445–52), and such a condemnation is justified by the behaviour of the two Spartans to appear in the drama, Menelaus, king of

Sparta, and his daughter Hermione. Whether or not Kitto is correct in seeing in the *Andromache* 'a violent attack on the Spartan mind, on *Machtpolitik*: in particular on three Spartan qualities, arrogance, treachery, and criminal ruthlessness', it remains true surely that Andromache's words are very much a product of the time when this play was first produced, years when Athens and Sparta were locked in a seemingly endless struggle whose ultimate purpose was the utter destruction of one of the two combatants.[10]

Patriotism, especially patriotism carried to the point when it qualifies as jingoism, is no longer fashionable today, and the Peloponnesian War has little meaning to us. It suggests an attitude of mind which applauds gunboat diplomacy and the sentiment 'my country right or wrong'. The combination of jingoism and poetic drama seems a most peculiar mixture, however much it was characteristic of both the Greek and Elizabethan theatre. Jingoism may be dead, but what of poetic drama—how is this to be restored to its rightful position?[11] T. S. Eliot has supplied an answer: 'What we have to do is to bring poetry into the world in which the audience lives and to which it returns when it leaves the theatre; not to transport the audience into some imaginary world totally unlike its own, an unreal world in which poetry is tolerated.'[12] Aeschylus, Sophocles and Euripides had the advantage over Eliot, for the society of which they were members, the society to be seen in fifth-century Athens, was part of a world where the spoken word was supreme, and the spoken word embraces the language of poetry as much as of prose. A tradition of prose literature had barely begun when Aeschylus wrote his plays, and it is only well into the second half of the fifth century that we meet, with the advent of the historians Herodotus and Thucydides, writers of prose to rival in subsequent reputation composers of dramatic and non-dramatic verse, and even Herodotus appears to have given public recitations of his writings. At school the Greek boy learned, naturally by heart, much poetry, concentrating on the works of Homer, and in the fourth century the philosopher Plato, for all his determination to censor the poetry available to the citizens of his ideal state, is capable of concocting a foundation myth to justify the tripartite division of responsibilities within his republic. Later in life the Greek might find his entertainment in the symposium or the theatre: at a symposium he would be expected to be able to fashion occasional verse in the form of scolia or drinking-songs; in the theatre, attending a comic performance, he would need an ear attuned to receive and appreciate linguistic and metrical nuances, if the parody of the comic writer was not to fall flat. Above all, the poet was not yet an 'artist' or an 'intellectual', divorced from and indifferent to the world which surrounded him. Sophocles, like Solon at Athens before him, was poet and politician, and, if Solon is a more distinguished figure in the political history of Athens, the poetic output of Sophocles was prodigious in quantity as well as in quality. Life changes, audiences change, and so do the interests of the dramatist. We are the heirs of the theatre of Ibsen and Chekhov, but that in itself should not blind us to the fact that there are other dramatic traditions and that these are equally valid.

NOTES

1 K. J. Dover, *Journal of Hellenic Studies* 77 (1957), p. 235.
2 The Theseus tradition is discussed by W. den Boer, *Greece and Rome* 16 (1969), pp. 1–13.
3 See G. E. M. de Ste. Croix, *The Origins of the Peloponnesian War* (London, 1972), p. 356 n. 1, on the date of the *Supplices*.
4 Greenwood, *Aspects of Euripidean Tragedy*, p. 107.
5 Ibid. p. 108.
6 Ibid. p. 109.
7 The translation quoted is that by Frank Jones in the Chicago series, *Euripides IV* (1958), pp. 71 and 101–102.
8 Greenwood, pp. 106 and 96.
9 I quote from the Chicago series (1955) the translation of the *Medea* by Rex Warner, pp. 87–88.
10 The interpretations of the *Andromache* are considered in the edition of that play by P. T. Stevens (Oxford, 1971), pp. 5ff.
11 See George Steiner, *The Death of Tragedy* (London, 1961), especially chapter VII, on tragic drama and verse.
12 *On Poetry and Poets*, p. 82.

Acting, actors, 5, 8, 11, 12, 15, 22–23, 25, 28–29, 32, 36–37, 42, 44ff., 59ff.
Adkins, A. W. H., 93 n. 2
Aesopus, 57
aetiology, 5
agon, 40–41
anabaden, 8
anachronism, 38, 94, 97, 99
Anthesteria, 5
aphrosyne, 40
arbitrator, 40, 42
Areopagus, 37, 48, 95
Arnott, Peter, 28, 43 n. 15
assembly, 26–27, 37–38, 42, 64, 94
Athene, as patron saint, 100
audience, 1–12, 18, 22–23, 26–27, 33, 40, 44, 52–53, 60, 64, 74, 76, 81, 98–99

Baldry, H. C., 21 n. 12
Barrett, W. S., 43 n. 21
Barton, Anne, 43 n. 14
Baumol, William J., 10 n. 1
Beckerman, Bernard, 43 n. 28
behaviour, formalized, 67
Bethell, S. L., 66–67, 75 n. 22
Bowen, William G., 10 n. 1
Bradbrook, M. C., 10 n. 3, 43 n. 6, 75 n. 3
Bradbury, Malcolm, 43 n. 11
break in performance, 17–18, 20
Burgess, Anthony, 31

Callippides, 44, 52
catharsis, 33
change of mind, 59, 61–62, 88
characters, number of speaking, 37
characters, stock, 54–58, 96
characterization, 53ff., 59ff., 76ff.
Chekhov, 7, 87, 103
chorus, 3–6, 11, 17–18, 20, 27, 29–31, 34, 37, 41, 44–46, 50, 54–55, 61, 69, 73, 92–93
Cleon, 39–40, 42, 66
Cocktail Party, The, 5
competition, 2–3, 10, 40, 43 n. 33, 44, 65
convention, 6–8, 10, 27ff., 51, 54ff., 59ff., 69ff.
costume, 8–9, 17–18, 45, 89–90
criticism of fellow-performers, 44

Dale, A. M., 43 n. 23, 43 n. 29, 59ff., 63ff.
Davison, J. A., 43 n. 10
Dawe, R. D., 61, 75 n. 7
debate on stage, 36–38, 40–41, 93, 99
Delebecque, É., 21 n. 3
Delium, battle of, 98
delivery, speed of, 22ff., 44
den Boer, W., 103 n. 2
description, verbal, 12, 46–49
de Ste. Croix, G.E.M., 103 n. 3
deus ex machina, 100
dianoia, 64–65

Dionysia, City, 2ff., 12ff., 28, 44, 73, 76, 94
Dionysia, Rural, 13
Dionysus, 1, 4–5, 14, 35
Dodds, E. R., 54–55, 58 n. 16, 75 n. 10
Dover, K. J., 93 n. 1, 103 n. 1
du Boulay, Juliet, 93 n. 4
Duchemin, Jacqueline, 43 n. 32

'ear world', 24, 32–33
Easterling, P. E., 75 n. 7
eccyclema, 9, 68
Edinburgh Festival, 2, 24
Eisenstein, Elizabeth L., 43 n. 11
Eliot, T. S., 5–6, 93, 102
Else, G. F., 29, 43 n. 16

family, 92
favour, reciprocity of, 99–100
film, 2, 7–8, 12, 18, 38, 69–70
Finnegan, Ruth, 75 n. 29
Fraenkel, Eduard, 61, 75 n. 6, 75 n. 26
Fry, Christopher, 5–6
Furies, appearance of, 34

Gellie, G. H., 75 n. 2
Goodlad, J. S. R., 10 n. 1
Goody, Jack, 43 n. 6
Gorgias, 40
Gould, John, 75 n. 23
Gould, John and Lewis, D.H., 13, 18, 21 n. 5, 21 n. 8, 21 n. 11, 45, 58 n. 4, 58 n. 5, 58 n. 14
Greene, W. C., 23
Greenwood, L. H. G., 70–71, 98, 100, 103 n. 4, 103 n. 8
Guthrie, W. K. G., 43 n. 31

Haigh, A. E., 13–14, 21 n. 4, 21 n. 8, 37, 43 n. 30, 45, 58 n. 3
hamilla, 40–41
Hamlet, 15, 23, 60
Hammond, N. G. L., 58 n. 9
Handley, E. W., 21 n. 1, 62, 75 n. 9
Harbage, Alfred, 10 n. 1, 46ff., 58 n. 6, 58 n. 7, 75 n. 17, 76
Harrison, A. R. W., 43 n. 33
Hart, Alfred, 19–20, 21 n. 13, 22, 42 n. 1, 42 n. 2, 45
Harvey, F. D., 24, 43 n. 9
Havelock, E. A., 23, 43 n. 6
Hawkes, Terence, 10 n. 4, 43 n. 6
Hippias, 40
Hourmouziades, N. C., 21 n. 5
Hubbard, M. E., 10 n. 12, 29
Hunningher, B., 21 n. 2

Ibsen, 7, 87, 103
imagination, power of individual, 32–35
improbability, 60ff., 88
interpolation, actors', 15, 31

Jaeger, Werner, 93 n. 7
Jebb, R. C., 61, 75 n. 5
jingoism, 96ff.
Jones, David E., 10 n. 6
Jones, John, 56–57, 58 n. 18, 93 n. 13
Joseph, B. L., 22, 42 n. 4, 58 n. 2, 65ff., 75 n. 16, 75 n. 17
Julius Caesar, 46

Kitto, H. D. F., 86, 102
Klein, David, 42 n. 4
Knox, B. M. W., 43 n. 13, 43 n. 14, 43 n. 24
Lattimore, Richmond, 93 n. 6, 93 n. 12
law-court, 26–27, 37–39, 41–42, 64, 94
leap on stage, 31–32
Lenaea, 16, 19
literacy, 24
liturgy, 1–2
Lloyd-Jones, Hugh, 75 n. 10, 86
logographos, 26
Lord, A. B., 43 n. 11
Lucas, D. W., 62, 75 n. 8
Lynch, J. P., 43 n. 12
'lyric-iambic sequence', 71

Macbeth, 60
McLuhan, Marshall, 24, 43 n. 11
marriage, arranged, 84–85, 98
Martin, Victor, 11–12
mask, 28, 45ff., 54–58
Maxwell-Stuart, P. G., 43 n. 27
'message', 8
motivation, 77–78
Murder in the Cathedral, 5, 93
Murray, Gilbert, 23, 93 n. 14
myth, 54, 59
mythology, Greek, 95

Neumann, Gerhard, 58 n. 11
New Comedy, 54, 62
Notopoulos, J. A., 75 n. 24

O'Connor, J. B., 58 n. 12
Ong, W. J., 43 n. 11
opera, 70–71
oral culture, 23ff., 65ff.
oral literature, African, 72
oral transmission, 95
origin of Greek drama, 28–29, 51
Othello, 23, 60

Paley, F. A., 43 n. 25, 70
Panathenaic festival, 28
parallels, mythological, 65
Parenti, Iride, 58 n. 12
Pathmanathan, R. Sri, 43 n. 26
performance, length of, 11–21, 21ff., 33, 44
peripeteia, 4
Pettet, E. B., 58 n. 1
'philosophy' and dramatists, 3–4, 76, 98

play, brevity of Greek, 11–12, 19, 53–54, 62
play, length of Elizabethan, 19–20
plot, 57, 59ff.
Polus, 42, 53
pursuit of gain, 79

Rabb, Theodore K., 43 n. 11
Raubitschek, A. E., 21 n. 9
reading and writing, 24–26
realism, 6–10, 27, 31, 34, 45ff., 52, 61–63, 68ff., 84ff., 94–96, 100
recognition (*anagnorisis*), 87–89
Rees, B. R., 10 n. 5, 43 n. 17
Reeve, M. D., 43 n. 23
religion, 4–5, 14, 28
reputation, 81, 99
revenge, 77–80, 82, 90, 99
rhapsode, 28–29, 51–52
rhetoric, 40, 42, 63ff.
ridicule, fear of, 97
Rockwell, Joan, 93 n. 1
Romeo and Juliet, 20, 23, 45

scenery, 47–48
sexuality, 81–83, 85, 92
Shakespeare, 15, 19, 22, 25, 27, 36, 41, 63, 66, 76, 94–95
Simpson, Michael, 75 n. 7
Solmsen, F., 93 n. 11
sophists, 40, 42, 65
Spartans, opponents of Athens, 101–2
speech, expository, 27, 98
speech, messenger, 6, 28ff., 38
Spitzbarth, Anna, 58 n. 15
stage properties, 46, 89–90
Stamm, Rudolph, 6
Stanford, W. B., 42 n. 3
Steiner, George, 103 n. 11
Stevens, P. T., 103 n. 10
stichomythia, 72
Stoll, E. E., 59–60, 75 n. 3
success, importance of, 77, 81, 97

television, 2, 12, 19, 23
texts, survival of, 15
theatre, Elizabethan, 6, 22, 27, 46–48, 74, 102
theatre, Greek, 12, 22, 25–27, 32–33, 37, 42, 45, 47, 51, 54, 74, 102
Theatre of Dionysus, 1–2, 16, 19, 21, 26, 42, 44
Theodectes, 42
Theodorus, 53
Thespis, 4, 28
Theseus, as national hero, 56, 96ff.
Thesmophoria, 9
time, obsession with, 13
time, true and dramatic, 19
tragedians, output of Greek, 19
Trendall, A.D., 58 n. 11
tyrant, typical tragedy-, 54–56, 97

values, contemporary, 76ff.
Vellacott, Philip, 75 n. 10
Vernant, Jean-Pierre, 43 n. 33
verse, use of, 6, 37, 68
Vickers, Brian, 10 n. 3
violence, attitude to, 79, 99
violence on stage, 6, 27ff.

Walcot, Peter, 93 n. 1
Waldock, A. J. A., 75 n. 3
Watt, Ian, 43 n. 6
weapons used on stage, 30–31, 35
Webster, T. B. L., 43 n. 18, 57, 58 n. 11,
    58 n. 19

Werre-de Haas, M., 21 n. 10
Willcock, Gladys D., 43 n. 8
Williams, Raymond, 7
women, position in society of, 56, 81ff.,
    90–92
word play, 27, 40–41
word, spoken and written, 4, 22ff., 64ff.,
    74, 102

Yates, F. A., 74, 75 n. 35

AELIAN
V.H. xiv. 40   58 n. 13

AESCHINES
Ctesiph. 76   21 n. 6
Timarchus 25–26   75 n. 19

AESCHYLUS
Agamemnon
   40–263   44
   555ff.   86
   681ff.   41
   810ff.   94
   813–16   94
   844–46   94
   1035ff.   69
   1050–51   69
   1060–61   69
   1072ff.   34
   1085–86   41
   1217–22   34
   1242–44   34
   1343ff.   33
   1428   50
Choephori
   32   50
   168ff.   88
   205ff.   88
   231ff.   88
   299–301   80
   309–14   80
   400–4   80
   560–64   70
   602ff.   83
   653ff.   70
   675   70
   734ff.   86
   919   83
   1048–50   34
   1058   34
   1061   34
Eumenides
   47–48   34
   48–49   34
   51   34
   52   34
   54   34
   55–56   34
   69   34
   183–84   34
   234   48
   235–43   48
   244ff.   48
   289ff.   95
   409   48
   410–12   34
   439–41   48
   446   48
   640–41   65
   640–42   37
   657ff.   37
   667–73   37–38
   669ff.   95

   736–40   37
   741–43   94
   762ff.   95
   990   34
Persae
   230–45   96
Prometheus Vinctus
   85–86   41
   561ff.   34
   887–93   85
Seven Against Thebes
   200–1   83
   230–32   83
   564   50
   829–30   41
Supplices
   118–19   69
   129–30   69
   365–69   94
   749   83
   903ff.   29
   911ff.   56
   995ff.   83
   1003–5   83

ARISTOPHANES
Acharnians
   19ff.   13
   100   70
   104   70
   393ff.   8
   399   8
   408   10 n. 10
   409   10 n. 10
   410–13   9
   412ff.   89
   729ff.   70
   860ff.   70
Birds
   786–89   18
   788   18
   1498–99   19
Clouds
   41ff.   85
   52   85
Frogs
   52–53   15
   303–4   25
   959ff.   87
   1126–28   15
   1172–73   15
Thesmophoriazusae
   39ff.   9
   96   9
   98   9
   136ff.   9
   148–52   9
   265   9

ARISTOTLE
Ath. Pol. 28.3   75 n. 20
Poetics
   1449a 14–15   36

1449a	24–28	68
1449b	21ff.	64
1449b	27	33
1450a	22	75 n. 1
1450b	16–20	24
1451a	38–b 11	96
1452b	12	29
1453a	17ff.	54
1453b	19–22	92
1454a	5–7	43 n. 19
1454a	22–24	56, 81
1454a	32–33	62
1454b	2–6	100
1454b	19ff.	88
1455a	4ff.	88
1455a	22–32	9–10
1455a	30–32	52
1456a	25–27	92
1456a	34–36	64
1456a	36–b 2	64
1460b	23–26	60
1461b	26ff.	51
1461b	33–35	44

Rhet.

1403b	33	75 n. 33

CICERO
de Oratore iii. 195–96   26
Orator   173   26
Tusc.   ii. 49–50   29

DEMETRIUS
On Style   195   43 n. 20

DEMOSTHENES
Meid.   74   21 n. 6

EURIPIDES
Alcestis

252ff.	34
259	34
323–25	64
1159–63	3–4

Andromache

42–44	29
147ff.	90
445–52	101
765	54
1284–88	3–4

Bacchae

176–77	90
180	90
205	90
249–54	90
501–2	34–35
507–8	41
827ff.	90
912ff.	90
918–22	35
1034	69
1043ff.	35
1168ff.	90
1388–92	3–4

Cyclops

145ff.	90

Electra

19ff.	90
43–44	86
55	89
57–59	89
75–76	86
77–78	89
107–9	89
185	89
220ff.	88
255	86
272–73	92
283	88
302ff.	89
304ff.	89
319ff.	87
343–44	90
364–65	86
367ff.	86
404–31	86
409ff.	89
508ff.	87–88
515ff.	88
532ff.	88
539ff.	88
558ff.	88
573–74	88
577–78	88
581–82	88
651ff.	89–90
932–33	90–91
966	89
1011ff.	41
1036–40	91
1052–53	91
1107	89
1249	85
1284	86

Hecuba

568–70	91
1056ff.	33
1132ff.	42
1145ff.	32
1187ff.	42

Helen

122	33
422	90
632–33	50
859–60	31
1079–81	90
1088	90
1186ff.	36
1186–87	90
1203	36
1251	36
1294–1300	36
1617–18	76
1688–92	3–4

Heraclidae

55ff.	29
269ff.	29

271	29	1032	91
273	29	1327ff.	36
320–28	100	1446ff.	5
476–77	83	*Medea*	
Hercules Furens		271ff.	101
130–32	50	350–51	101
922ff.	35	459ff.	41
969–70	31	465–519	41
1169–71	100	468	41
1220–25	100	522	38
1336–37	100	522–75	41
1404–5	100	546	41
Hippolytus		663ff.	100–101
10–11	87	717–18	101
307–9	87	721	101
337–43	87	730	101
351	87	731–45	101
373ff.	87	824–45	101
462–66	79–80	1416–19	3–4
581	87	*Orestes*	
700	77	108	91
856ff.	90	211ff.	50
962–63	87	219–20	50
967–69	92	223–26	50
986–87	38	253ff.	35, 50
990–91	38	259	35
1022	38	268ff.	35
1025–26	38	272	35
1347ff.	50	385	50
1392ff.	50	387	50
1455	87	389	50
Ion		408	35
398–400	91	491ff.	38
510–65	72–73	552–56	38
515–16	31	605–6	91
524	30	640–41	27
530–62	73	866ff.	38
661–63	41	887ff.	38
666–67	92	898ff.	38
670–75	100	902ff.	38
757–807	92	917ff.	38
843–46	91	932ff.	38
1046–47	79	1366–68	31
1122ff.	35–36	1369ff.	31
1196–1208	36	1385	69
1250ff.	29	1519	30
1575ff.	100	1575	30
Iphigenia in Aulis		1608	30
34ff.	90	*Phoenissae*	
304ff.	30	88ff.	91
309ff.	30	310–2	69
315	30	452ff.	42
317	30	636–37	41
319	30	679	69
381	50	680	69
480ff.	62	1301	69
1252	62	1487–88	50
1368ff.	62	1493	41
1394	91	1660–61	29
Iphigenia in Tauris		*Rhesus*	
281ff.	35	208ff.	90
727ff.	90	294–97	69
958–60	5	510–11	77

	527ff.	19	222	72
	627–41	68–69	xvi. 125	75 n. 21
	793ff.	29	*Odyssey*	
Supplices			iv. 274ff.	51
	40–41	91	vi. 180–85	85
	187–88	101	viii. 521ff.	52
	195–249	98	xiii. 187ff.	76
	201–28	98	256ff.	76
	229ff.	98	267–70	77
	238ff.	98	xxii. 373–74	79
	253–56	98	411–16	79
	337ff.	98	475–77	79
	361–64	99	*Hymn to Aphrodite*	
	403ff.	97	113–16	69
	409ff.	40	*Hymn to Apollo*	
	426	99	162–63	51
	426ff.	40		
	427–28	40, 99	'LONGINUS'	
	438–39	99	*On Sublimity*	
	458–62	99	i. 4	75 n. 4
	566–67	99		
	707ff.	99	MENANDER	
	759ff.	99	*Dyskolos*	
	942–46	99	58–68	84–85
	1014ff.	31	249–54	62
	1169–75	99	302ff.	62
	1176–79	100	315ff.	62
	1185ff.	100	841	62
	1213–26	100		
Trojan Women			PLATO	
	643–56	83–84, 91	*Gorgias*	
	655–56	91	502b	10 n. 2
	657ff.	91–92	502c–d	42
	665–66	92	*Ion*	
	914ff.	40	535c	52
	966–68	40	535e	52
	969ff.	40	*Laws*	
	989–90	40	659a–c	3
Frag. 189 (Nauck²)		43 n. 32	*Phaedrus*	
			275d–277a	25
FRONTO			*Republic*	
de Eloqu. i. 17		58 n. 19	392eff.	51
			398a	52
A. GELL.			605c–606b	33
vi. 5		53		
			PLUTARCH	
HERODOTUS			*Moralia*	
iii. 80		56	79 B	75 n. 15
			334 A	58 n. 13
HESIOD			998 E	43 n. 19
Theogony 154ff.		82	*Vit. X orat.*	
	166	82	841 F	15
	172	82		
	176–78	82	QUINTILIAN	
	570ff.	81–82	xi. 3. 73	58 n. 19
Works and Days			xi. 3. 123	75 n. 21
	90ff.	82	xi. 3. 157ff.	75 n. 28
HOMER			SOPHOCLES	
Iliad			*Ajax*	
	iii. 213	71	292–93	83
	214	72	296ff.	49
			348ff.	49

430–33	41
658ff.	90
815ff.	49, 90
915–19	49–50
1024ff.	90
1042	46
1047ff.	41
1163	41
1226ff.	41
1411–13	50

Antigone

36	56
163ff.	55
221–22	55
280ff.	55
289ff.	55
305ff.	56
441ff.	55–56
489ff.	56
526	45
526ff.	36
527	45
531ff.	56
531–35	36
536–60	36
561–62	36
563ff.	36
569	56
572	36
574	36
726ff.	56
760–61	56
773–80	56
803	46
889f.	61
905–12	40
1033ff.	56
1040	61
1091ff.	61
1232	67

Electra

4ff.	12
47–48	80
54–58	90
61	80
516ff.	41
757ff.	90
837ff.	83
959–85	81
989	81
997–98	81

Oedipus Coloneus

14–15	48
16–18	48
24	48
39–40	48
42	48
58–61	48
66	97
72	97
287–88	97
299ff.	97
319–20	50

337–41	83
562–68	97
579ff.	97
668ff.	48
818ff.	30
845	30
902–3	97
913–14	97
960ff.	27
1096ff.	30
1115–18	30
1139ff.	30
1284ff.	27
1422–23	97
1624–25	50

Oedipus Tyrannus

1–8	47
15–16	47
19–21	47
32	47
78–79	46
81	46, 50
82–83	46
137–41	55
334ff.	55
346–49	55
378	55
385ff.	55
399–400	55
437	55
523–24	55
555–56	55
577ff.	55
622–23	55
779–80	55
800ff.	55
813	55
1005–6	79
1062ff.	55
1076ff.	55
1152–66	55

Philoctetes

7	49
86–95	80
88	81
234ff.	49
530ff.	49
696ff.	49
732ff.	49
783–84	49
821–26	47, 49
927ff.	49
1000ff.	31
1004ff.	49
1081ff.	49
1299	30–31

Trachiniae

1ff.	82
24–25	82
27–31	82
69–71	82
189–91	79
230–31	81

248ff.	78
254–57	78
260–76	78
277–78	78
278–79	78
280	78
307ff.	39
351ff.	39, 82
354–55	82
400ff.	39
425–26	39
431–33	39
436ff.	39, 82
497–530	82
562ff.	82–83
596–97	79
707ff.	79
719–22	81
765ff.	49
964ff.	49
983ff.	49

Frag. 442 (Pearson)   43 n. 21
Vit. Soph.
    4   75 n. 14
    14   75 n. 32

TIMOTHEUS
Persae   162ff.   69

THUCYDIDES
    iii. 38   39–40

VITRUVIUS
de Architectura
    v. 3–8   75 n. 34
    v. 6. 2   74

XENOPHON
Oeconomicus
    iii. 7   21 n. 7
Sym.   iii. 11   52–53

DATE DUE

AP 28 '88			
GAYLORD			PRINTED IN U.S.A.